SUPER EASY SONGBOOK

BEAUTIFUL BALLA

T0086954

ISBN 978-1-70515-464-9

HAL•LEONARD®

Visit Hal Leonard Online at
www.halleonard.com

Contact us:
Hal Leonard
7777 West Bluemound Road
Milwaukee, WI 53213
Email: info@halleonard.com

In Europe, contact:
Hal Leonard Europe Limited
42 Wigmore Street
Marylebone, London, W1U 2RN
Email: info@halleonardeurope.com

In Australia, contact:
Hal Leonard Australia Pty. Ltd.
4 Lentara Court
Cheltenham, Victoria, 3192 Australia
Email: info@halleonard.com.au

All of Me

Words and Music by John Stephens
and Toby Gad

Moderately slow

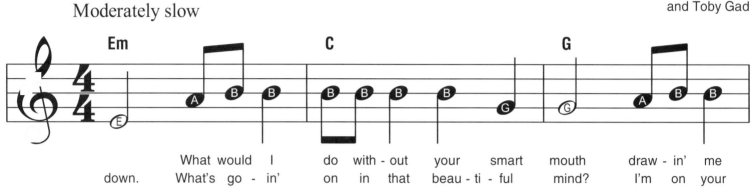

What would I do with-out your smart mouth draw-in' me
down. What's go - in' on in that beau-ti-ful mind? I'm on your

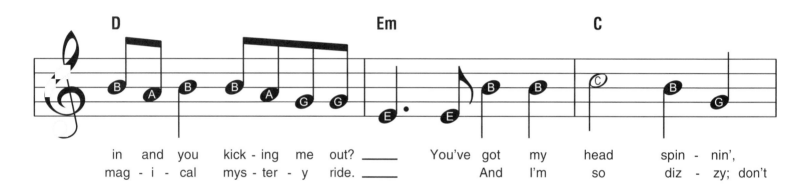

in and you kick-ing me out? _____ You've got my head spin-nin',
mag-i-cal mys-ter-y ride. _____ And I'm so diz-zy; don't

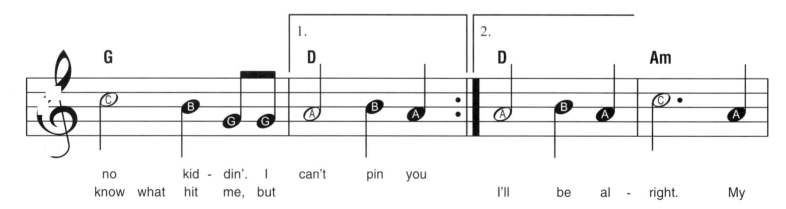

no kid-din'. I can't pin you
know what hit me, but I'll be al-right. My

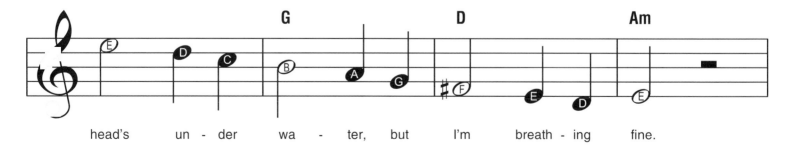

head's un-der wa-ter, but I'm breath-ing fine.

Always on My Mind

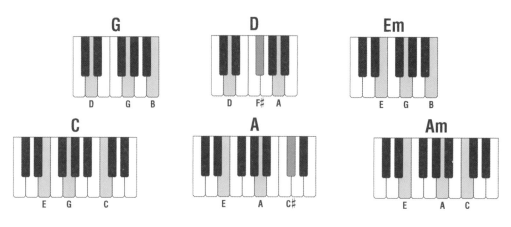

Words and Music by Wayne Thompson,
Mark James and Johnny Christopher

Moderately

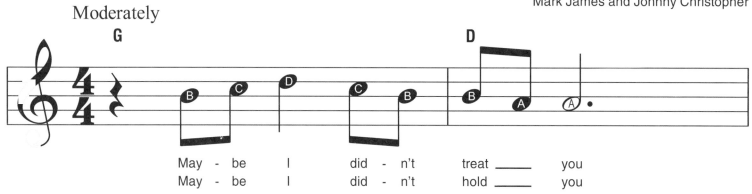

May - be I did - n't treat _____ you
May - be I did - n't hold _____ you

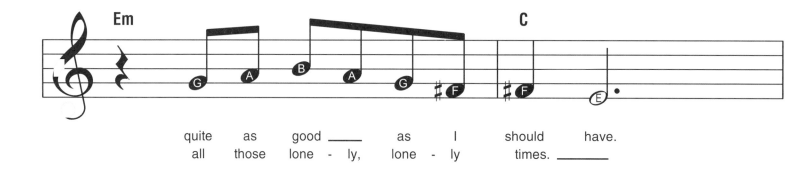

quite as good _____ as I should have.
all those lone - ly, lone - ly times. _____

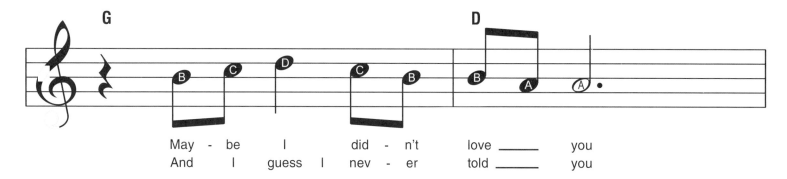

May - be I did - n't love _____ you
And I guess I nev - er told _____ you

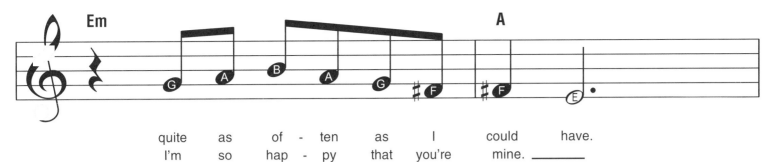

quite as of - ten as I could have.
I'm so hap - py that you're mine. _____

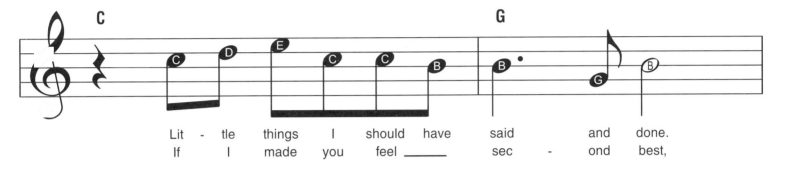

Lit - tle things I should have said and done.
If I made you feel _____ sec - ond best,

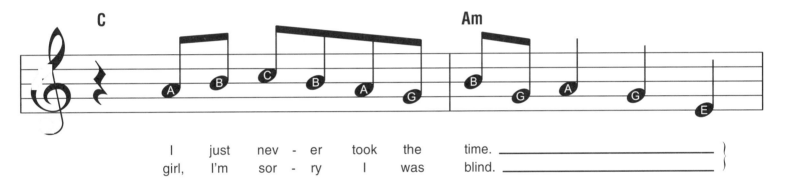

I just nev - er took the time. _____
girl, I'm sor - ry I was blind. _____

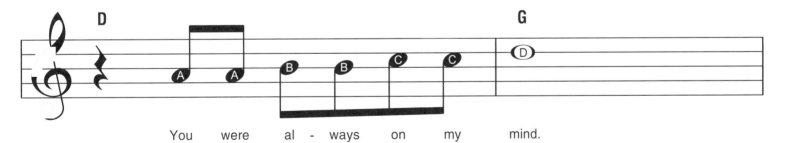

You were al - ways on my mind.

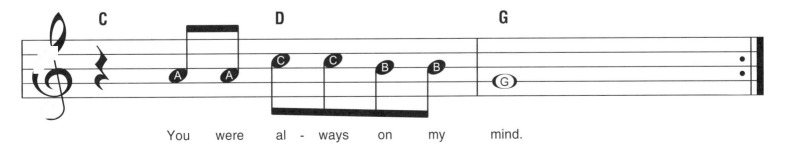

You were al - ways on my mind.

And So It Goes

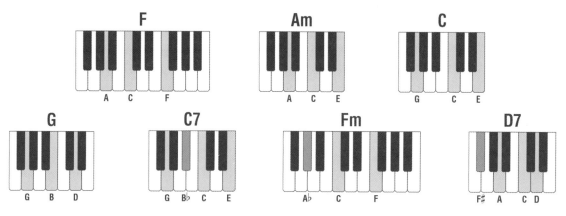

Words and Music by
Billy Joel

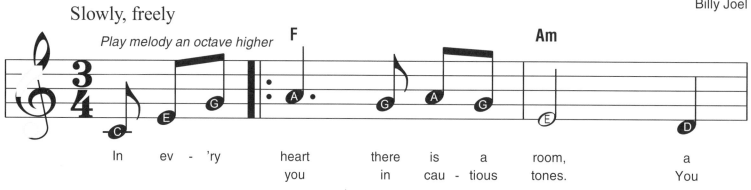

Slowly, freely

Play melody an octave higher

In ev - 'ry heart there is a room, a
you in cau - tious tones. You

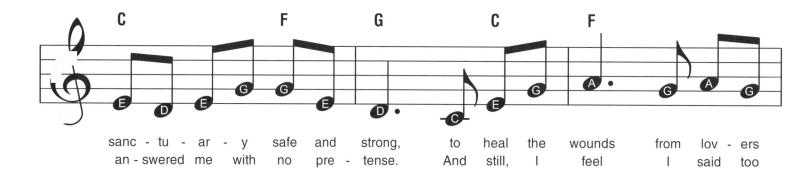

sanc - tu - ar - y safe and strong, to heal the wounds from lov - ers
an - swered me with no pre - tense. And still, I feel I said too

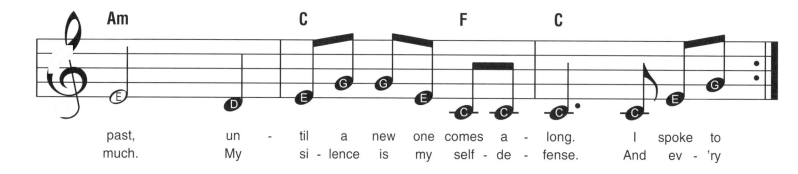

past, un - til a new one comes a - long. I spoke to
much. My si - lence is my self - de - fense. And ev - 'ry

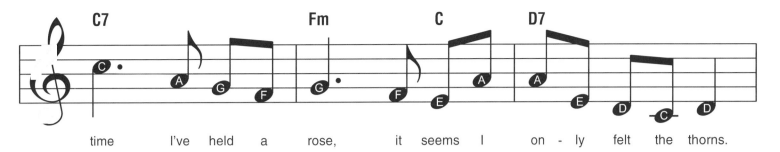

time I've held a rose, it seems I on - ly felt the thorns.

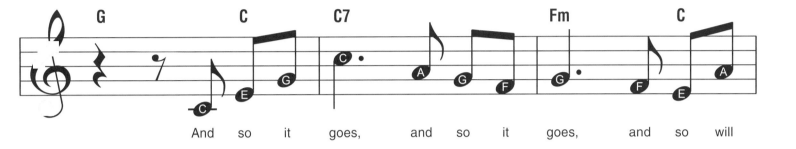

And so it goes, and so it goes, and so will

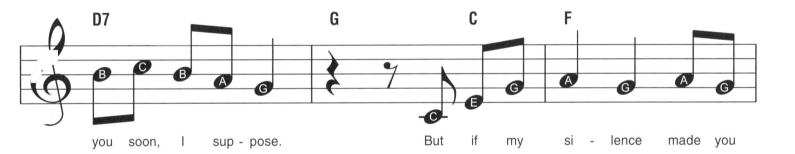

you soon, I sup - pose. But if my si - lence made you

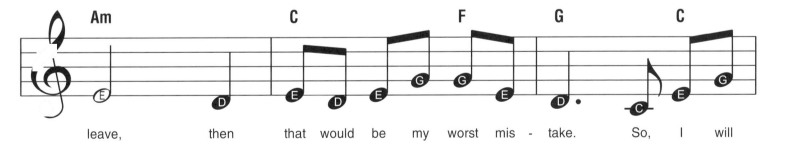

leave, then that would be my worst mis - take. So, I will

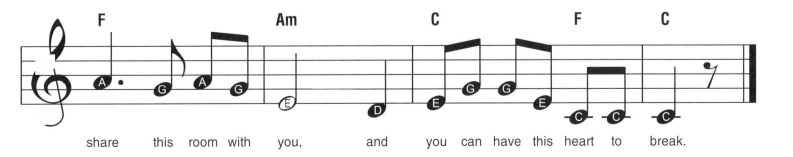

share this room with you, and you can have this heart to break.

Angel

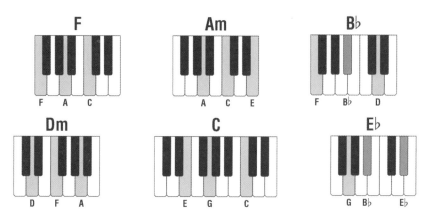

Words and Music by
Sarah McLachlan

Gently

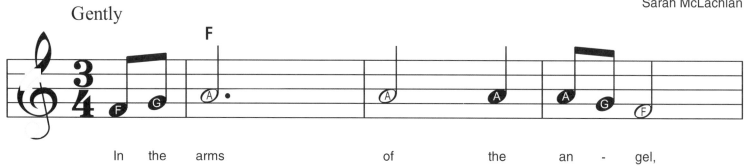

In the arms of the an - gel,

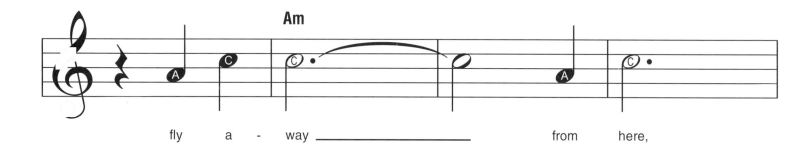

fly a - way _____ from here,

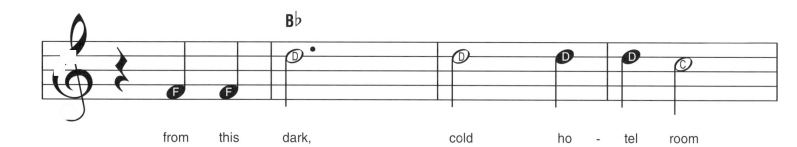

from this dark, cold ho - tel room

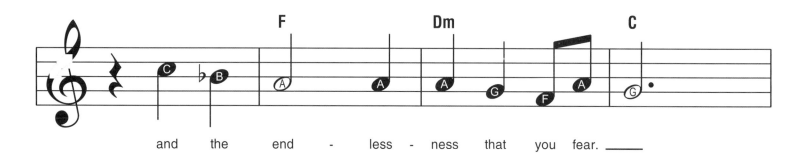

and the end - less - ness that you fear. _____

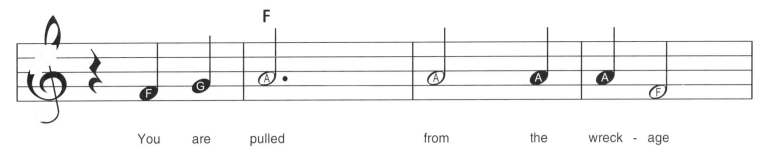

You are pulled from the wreck - age

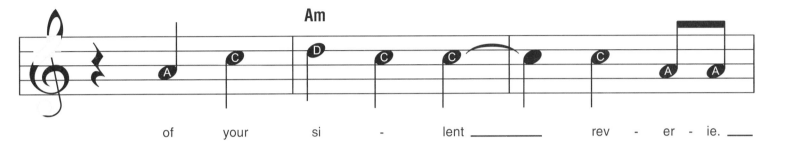

of your si - lent _____ rev - er - ie. ____

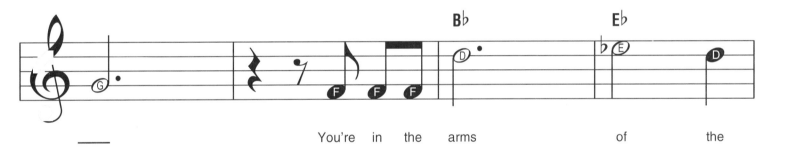

____ You're in the arms of the

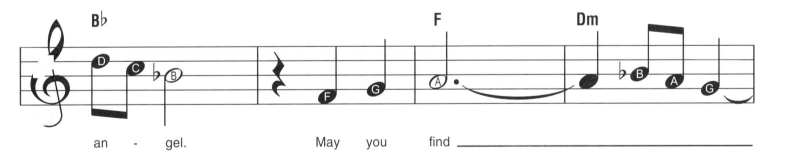

an - gel. May you find _____

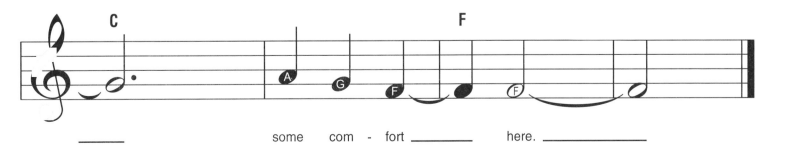

_____ some com - fort _____ here. _____

Annie's Song

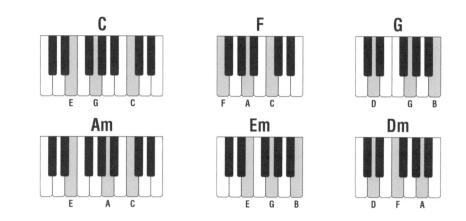

Words and Music by
John Denver

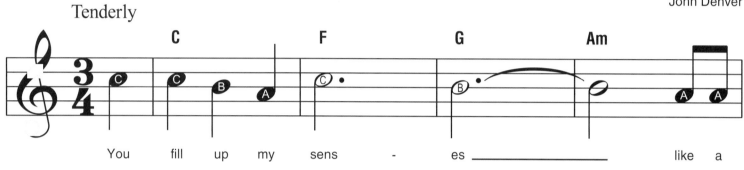

Tenderly

You fill up my sens - es ___ like a

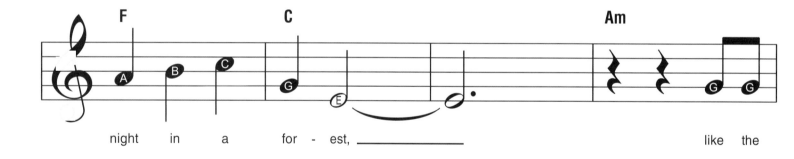

night in a for - est, ___ like the

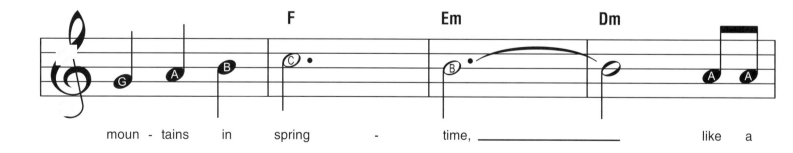

moun - tains in spring - time, ___ like a

walk in the rain. _____ Like a

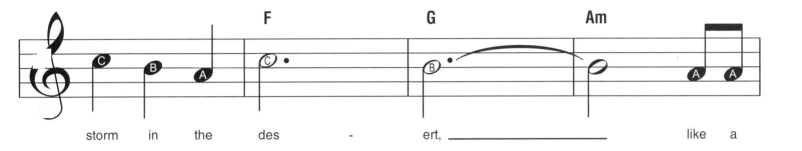

storm in the des - ert, _____ like a

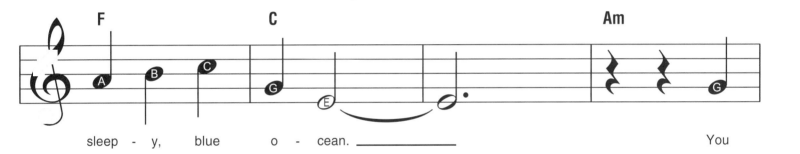

sleep - y, blue o - cean. _____ You

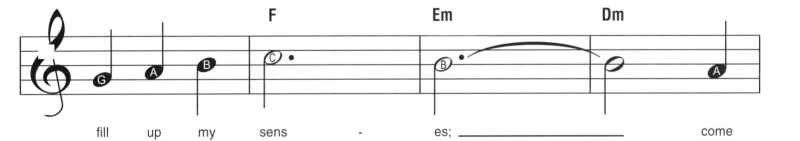

fill up my sens - es; _____ come

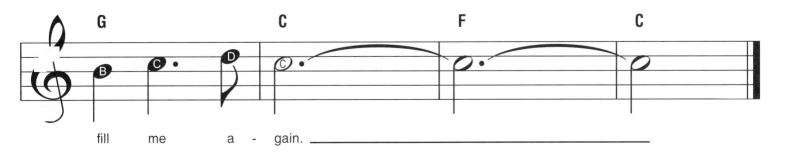

fill me a - gain. _____

As If We Never Said Goodbye

from SUNSET BOULEVARD

Music by Andrew Lloyd Webber
Lyrics by Don Black and Christopher Hampton,
with contributions by Amy Powers

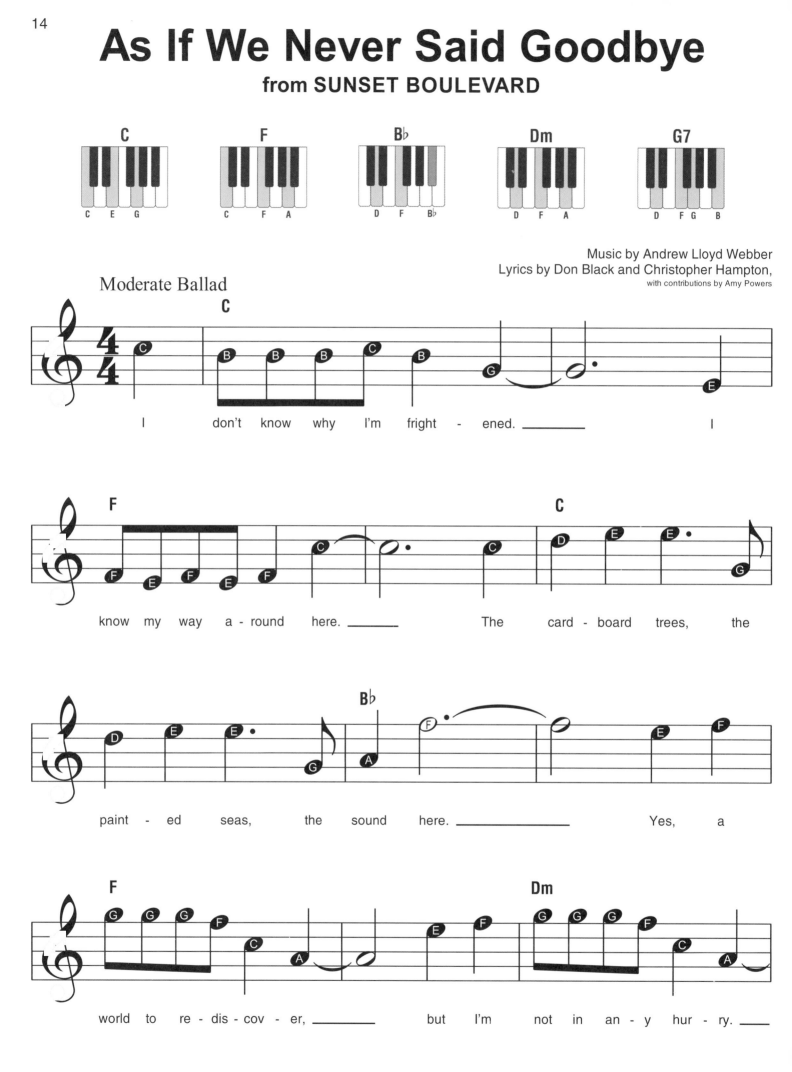

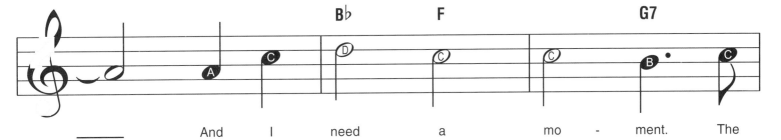

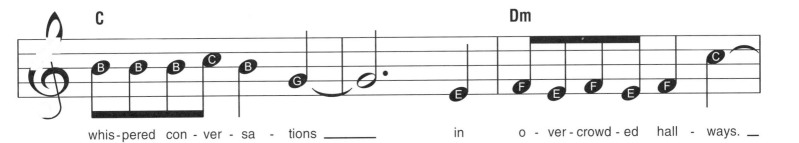

And I need a mo - ment. The

whis-pered con - ver - sa - tions _____ in o - ver - crowd - ed hall - ways. _

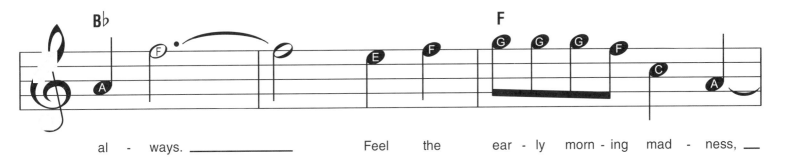

_____ The at - mos - phere as thrill - ing here as

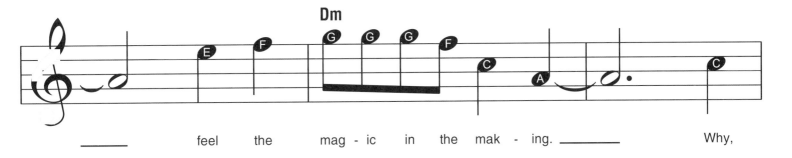

al - ways. _____ Feel the ear - ly morn - ing mad - ness, _

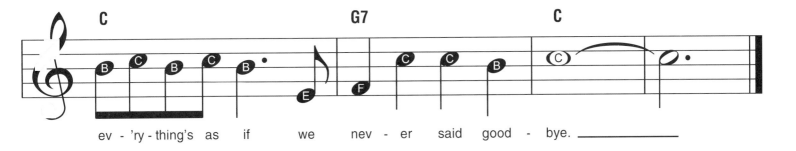

_____ feel the mag - ic in the mak - ing. _____ Why,

ev - 'ry - thing's as if we nev - er said good - bye. _____

At Last
from ORCHESTRA WIVES

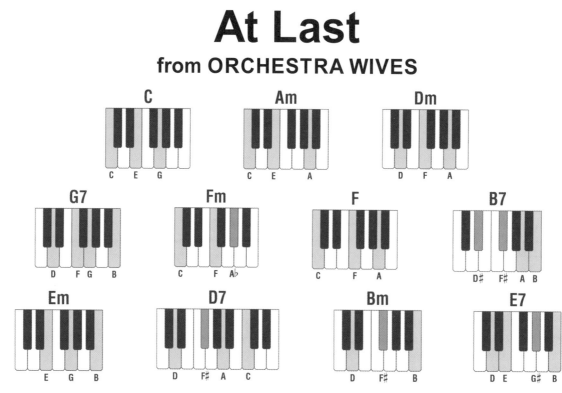

Lyric by Mack Gordon
Music by Harry Warren

Slow Shuffle

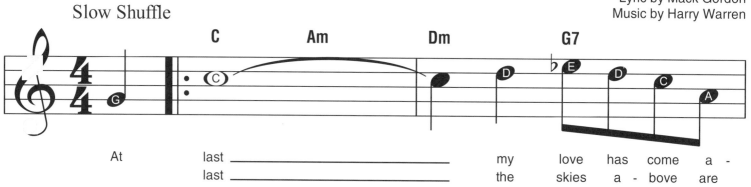

At last _____ my love has come a -
last _____ the skies a - bove are

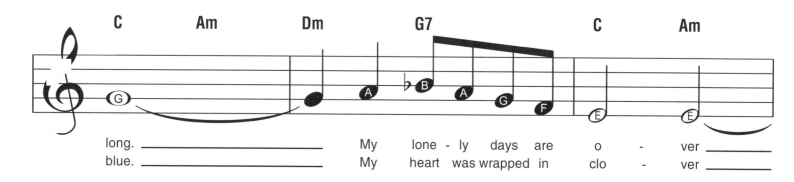

long. _____ My lone - ly days are o - ver _____
blue. _____ My heart was wrapped in clo - ver _____

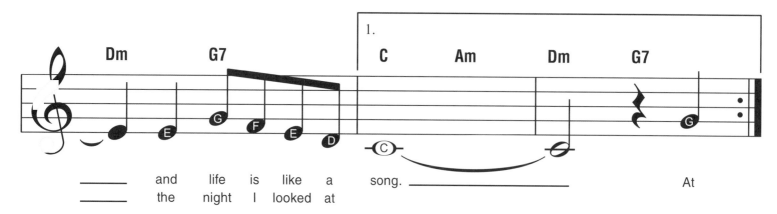

_____ and life is like a song. _____ At
_____ the night I looked at

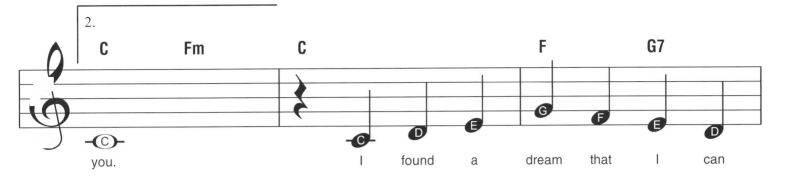

you. I found a dream that I can

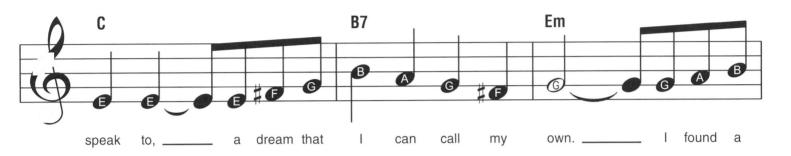

speak to, _____ a dream that I can call my own. _____ I found a

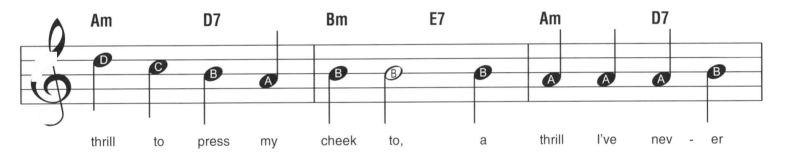

thrill to press my cheek to, a thrill I've nev - er

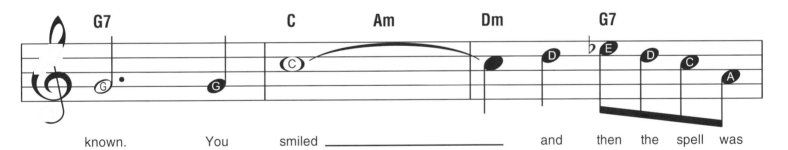

known. You smiled _____ and then the spell was

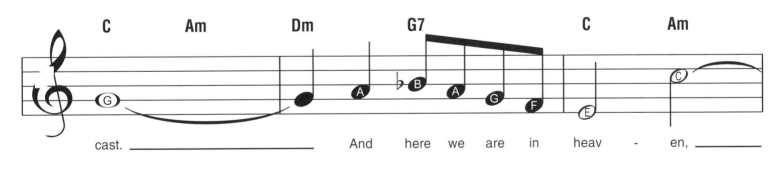

cast. _____ And here we are in heav - en, _____

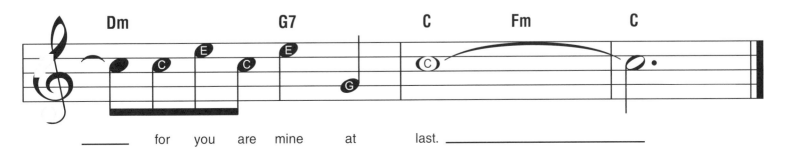

_____ for you are mine at last. _____

Colors of the Wind
from POCAHONTAS

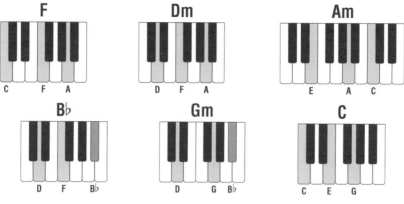

Music by Alan Menken
Lyrics by Stephen Schwartz

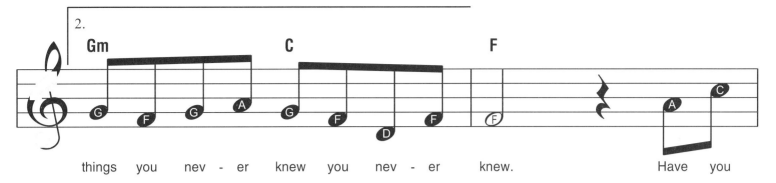

things you nev - er knew you nev - er knew. Have you

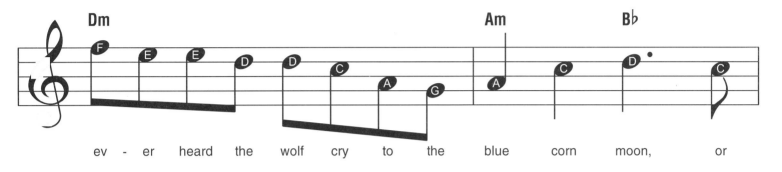

ev - er heard the wolf cry to the blue corn moon, or

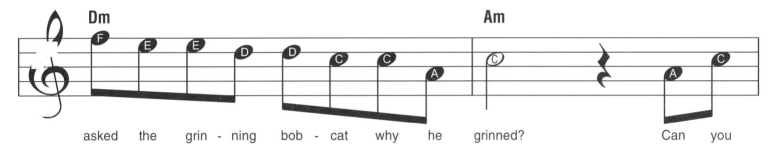

asked the grin - ning bob - cat why he grinned? Can you

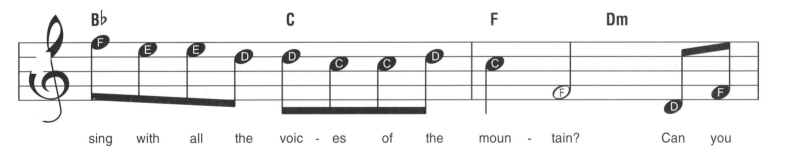

sing with all the voic - es of the moun - tain? Can you

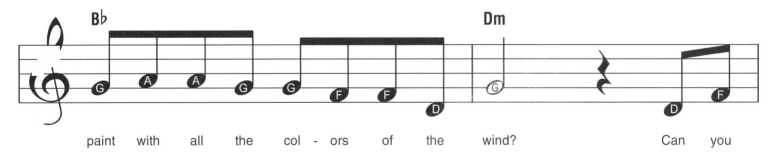

paint with all the col - ors of the wind? Can you

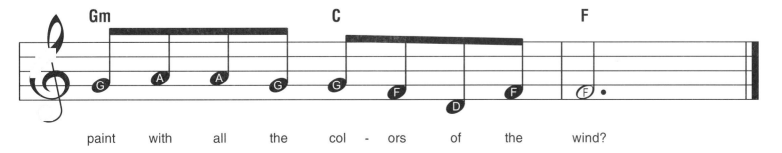

paint with all the col - ors of the wind?

Don't Cry for Me Argentina

from EVITA

Words by Tim Rice
Music by Andrew Lloyd Webber

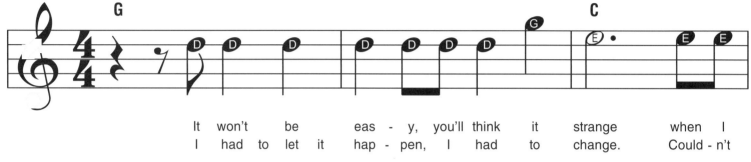

Slowly

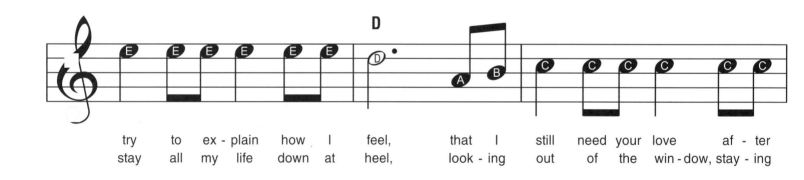

It won't be   eas - y, you'll think   it   strange   when I
I had to let it   hap - pen, I had   to   change.   Could - n't

try   to ex - plain how   I   feel,   that I   still   need your love   af - ter
stay   all   my life down at   heel,   look - ing   out   of the   win - dow, stay - ing

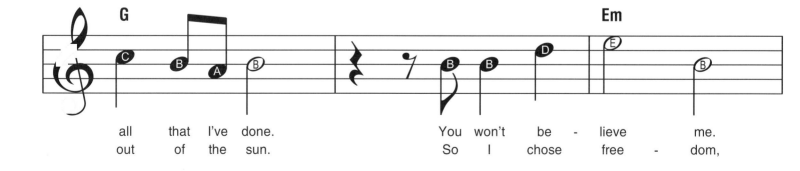

all   that   I've done.   You won't be - lieve   me.
out   of   the   sun.   So   I   chose   free - dom,

All you will see is a girl you once knew, al - though she's dressed up to the
run - ning a - round try - ing ev - 'ry - thing new, but noth - ing im - pressed me at

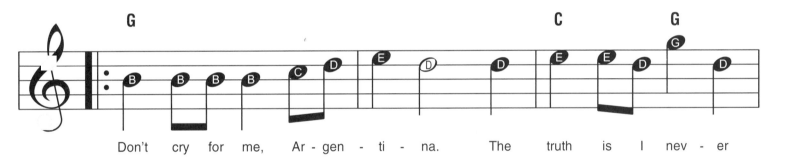

nines at six - es and sev - ens with you.
all. I nev - er ex - pect - ed it to.

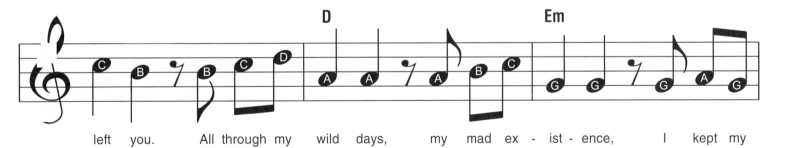

Don't cry for me, Ar - gen - ti - na. The truth is I nev - er

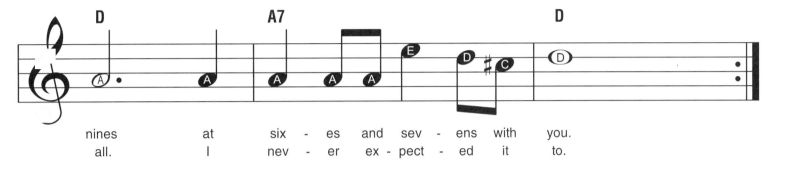

left you. All through my wild days, my mad ex - ist - ence, I kept my

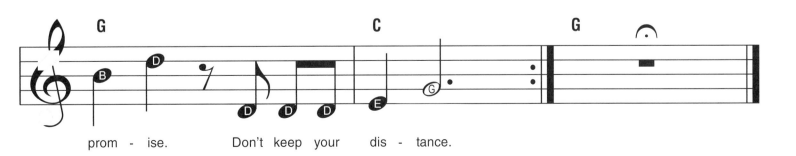

prom - ise. Don't keep your dis - tance.

Don't Let the Sun Go Down on Me

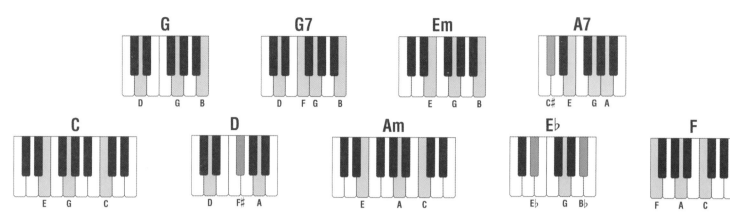

Words and Music by Elton John
and Bernie Taupin

Slow half-time feel

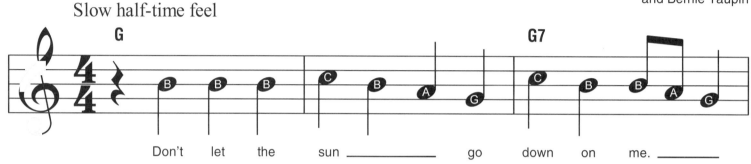

Don't let the sun _____ go down on me. _____

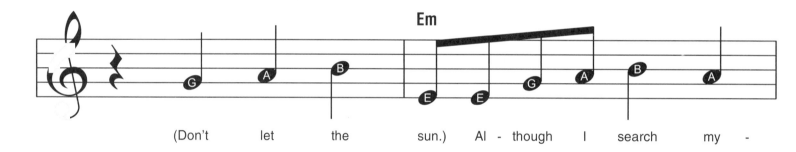

(Don't let the sun.) Al - though I search my -

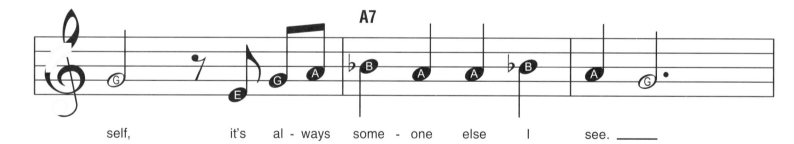

self, it's al - ways some - one else I see. _____

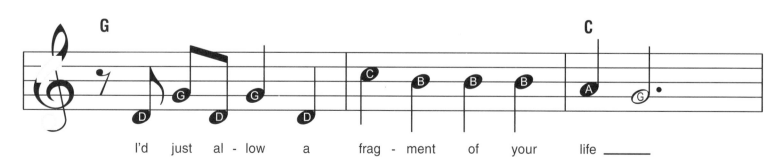

I'd just al - low a frag - ment of your life _____

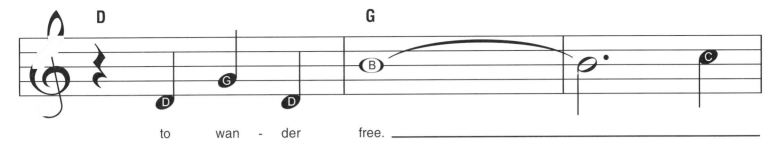

to wan - der free. _____

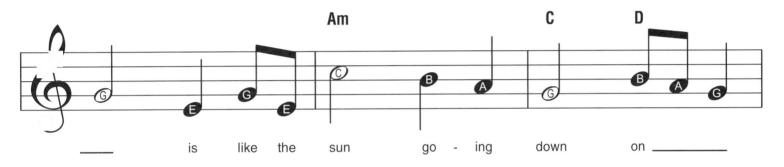

But los - ing ev - 'ry - thing ___

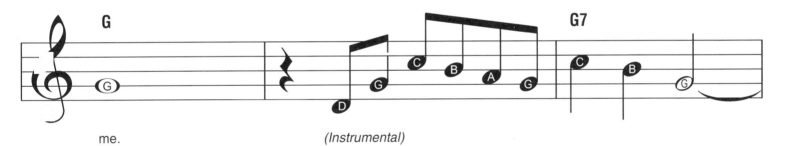

___ is like the sun go - ing down on _____

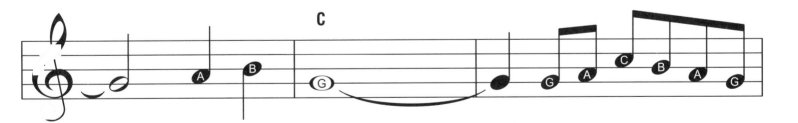

me. (Instrumental)

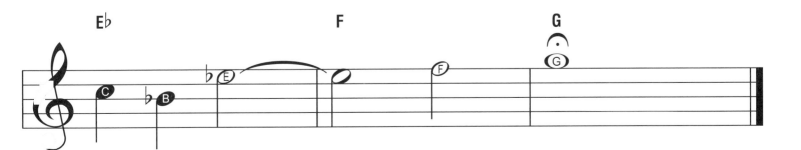

Evermore
from BEAUTY AND THE BEAST

Music by Alan Menken
Lyrics by Tim Rice

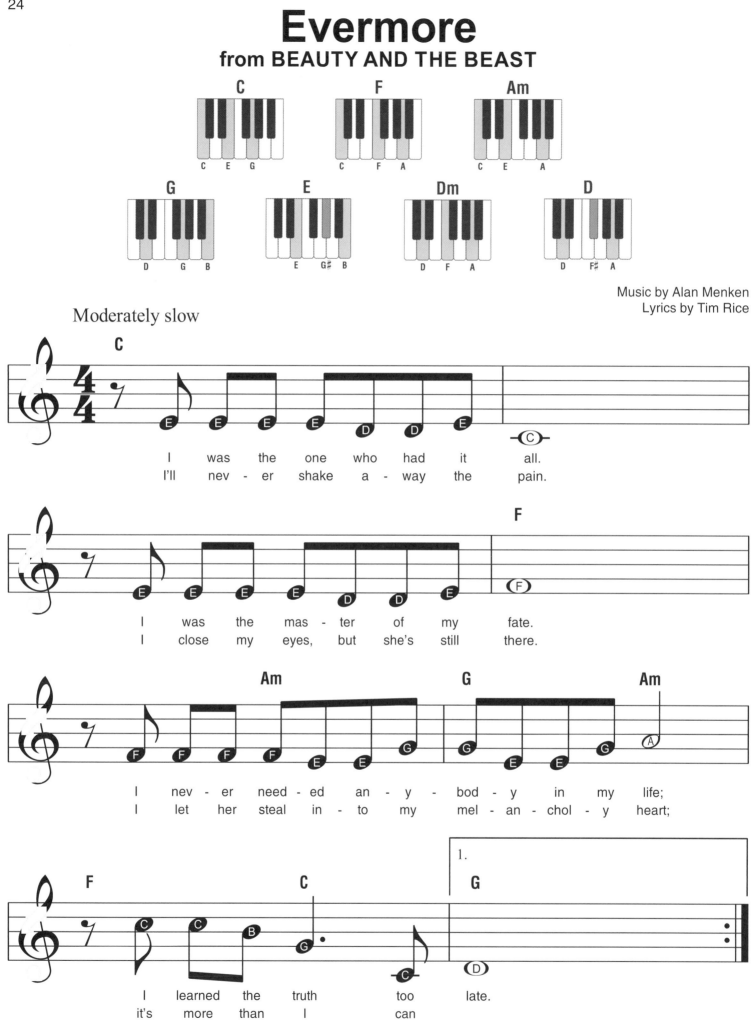

25

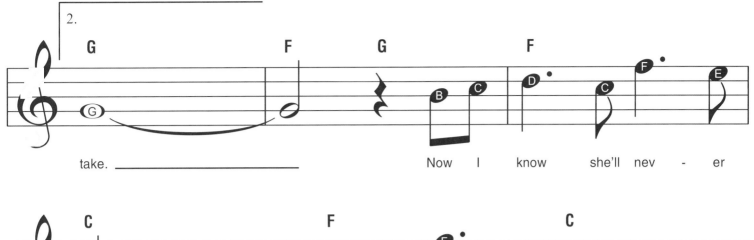

take. _____ Now I know she'll nev - er

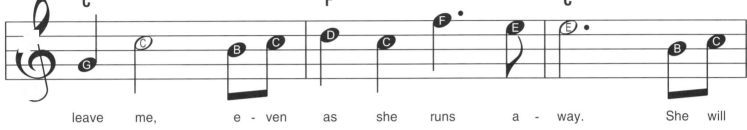

leave me, e - ven as she runs a - way. She will

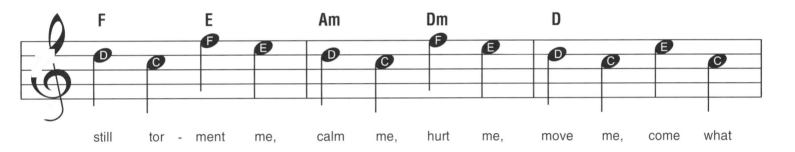

still tor - ment me, calm me, hurt me, move me, come what

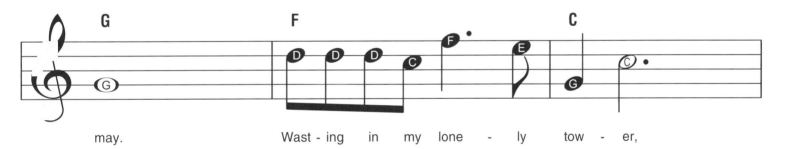

may. Wast - ing in my lone - ly tow - er,

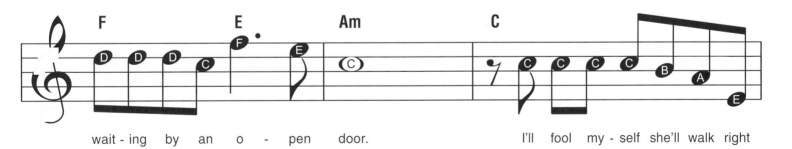

wait - ing by an o - pen door. I'll fool my - self she'll walk right

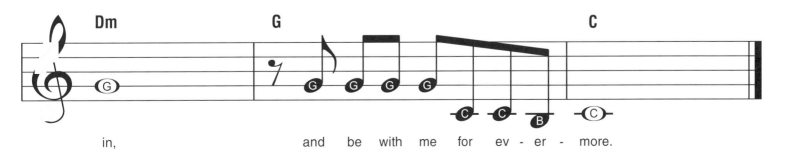

in, and be with me for ev - er - more.

Glory of Love
Theme from KARATE KID PART II

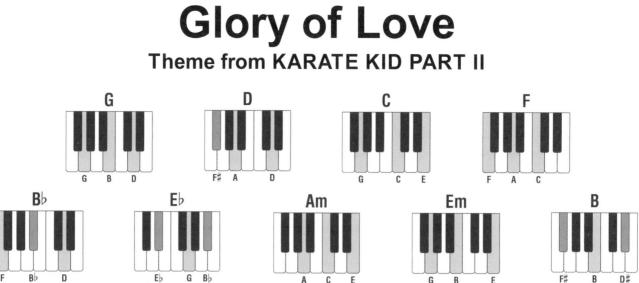

Words and Music by David Foster,
Peter Cetera and Diane Nini

Moderately

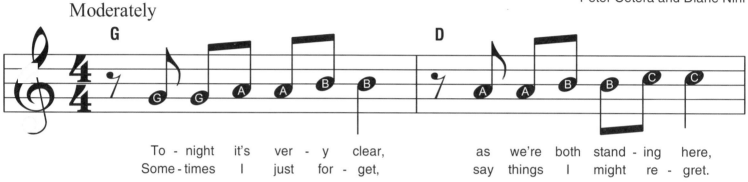

To - night it's ver - y clear, as we're both stand - ing here,
Some - times I just for - get, say things I might re - gret.

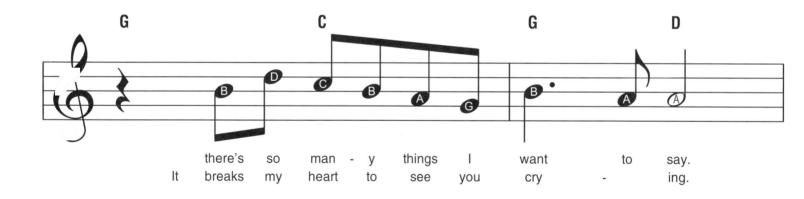

there's so man - y things I want to say.
It breaks my heart to see you cry - ing.

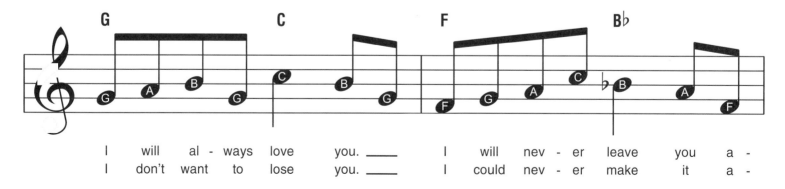

I will al - ways love you. _____ I will nev - er leave you a -
I don't want to lose you. _____ I could nev - er make it a -

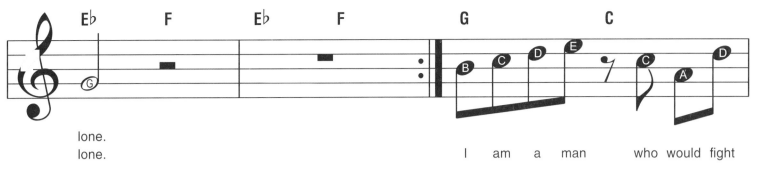

lone.
lone.   I   am   a   man   who would fight

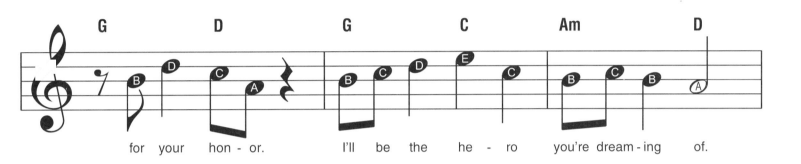

for   your   hon - or.   I'll   be   the   he - ro   you're dream - ing   of.

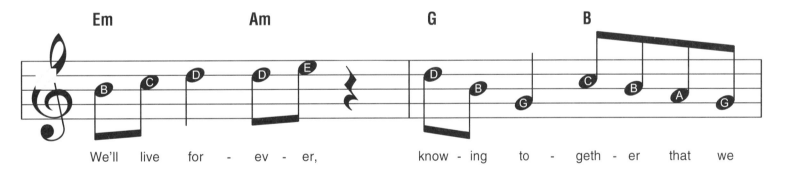

We'll   live   for - ev - er,   know - ing   to - geth - er   that   we

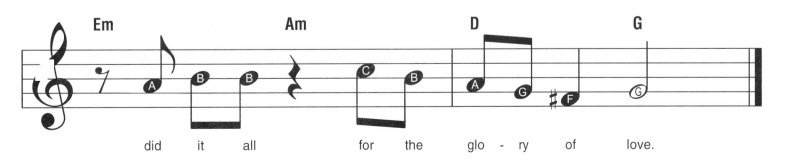

did   it   all   for   the   glo - ry   of   love.

Hallelujah

Words and Music by
Leonard Cohen

29

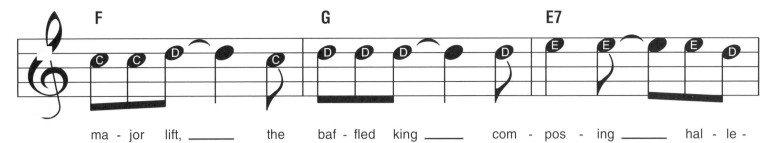

ma - jor lift, _____ the baf - fled king _____ com - pos - ing _____ hal - le -

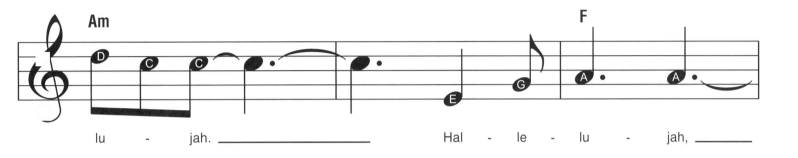

lu - jah. _____ Hal - le - lu - jah, _____

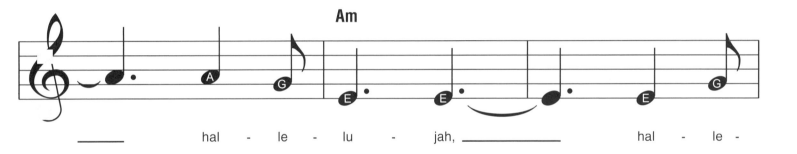

_____ hal - le - lu - jah, _____ hal - le -

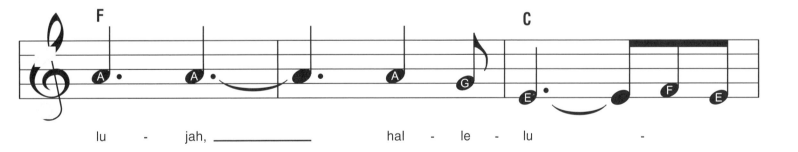

lu - jah, _____ hal - le - lu -

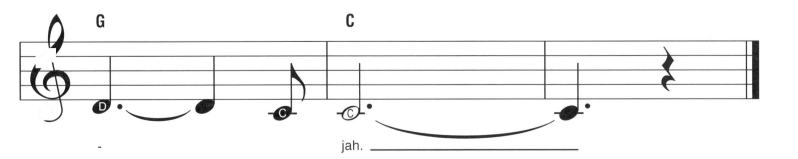

- jah. _____

Have I Told You Lately

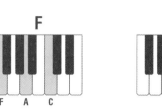
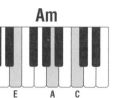
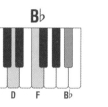
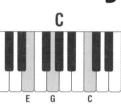
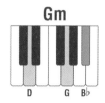

Words and Music by
Van Morrison

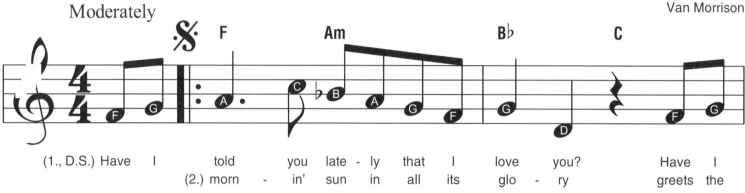

(1., D.S.) Have I told you late-ly that I love you? Have I
(2.) morn - in' sun in all its glo - ry greets the

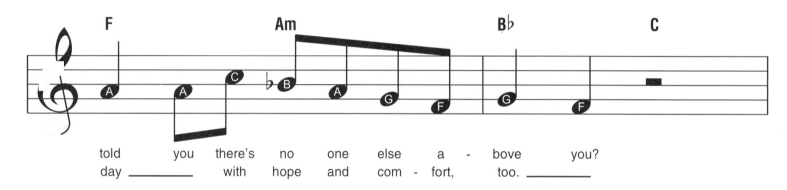

told you there's no one else a - bove you?
day _____ with hope and com - fort, too. _____

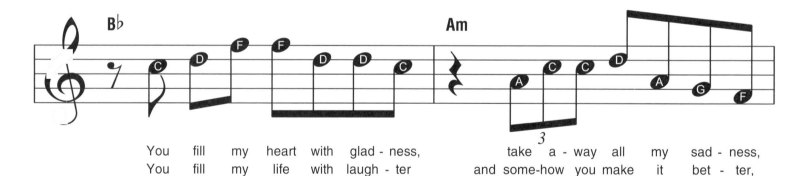

You fill my heart with glad - ness, take a - way all my sad - ness,
You fill my life with laugh - ter and some-how you make it bet - ter,

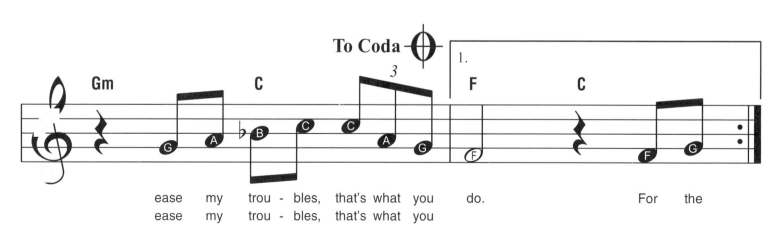

ease my trou - bles, that's what you do. For the
ease my trou - bles, that's what you

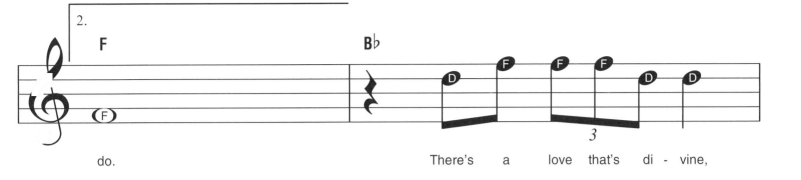

do.   There's   a   love that's di - vine,

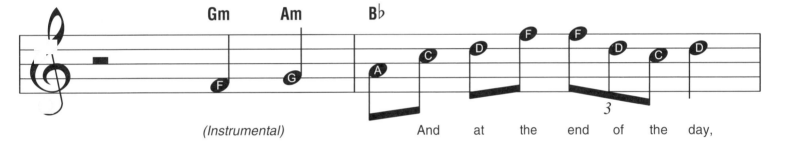

and   it's   yours and   it's   mine, _____   like   the sun.

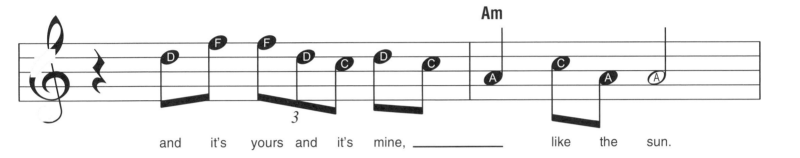

(Instrumental)   And   at   the   end   of   the day,

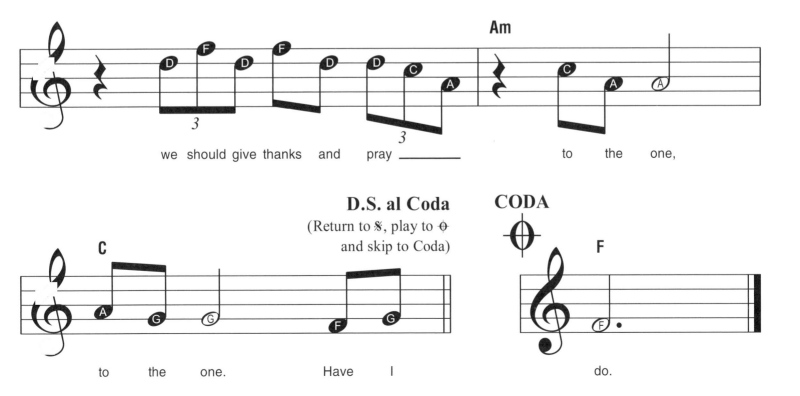

we   should give thanks and   pray _____   to   the one,

D.S. al Coda
(Return to 𝄋, play to ⊕
and skip to Coda)

CODA

to   the one.   Have   I   do.

Here, There and Everywhere

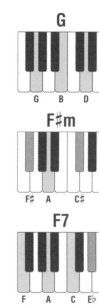
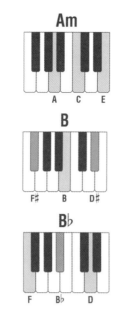
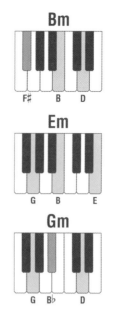
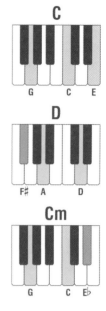

Words and Music by John Lennon
and Paul McCartney

Moderately

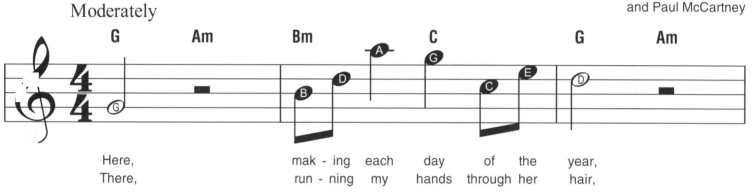

Here,
mak - ing each day of the year,

There,
run - ning my hands through her hair,

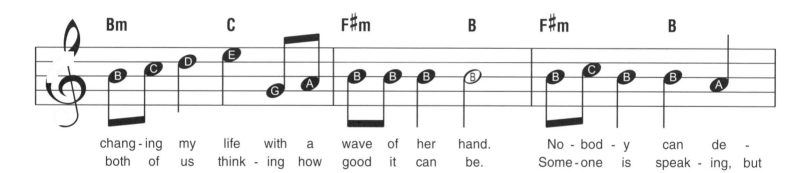

chang - ing my life with a wave of her hand.
No - bod - y can de -

both of us think - ing how good it can be.
Some - one is speak - ing, but

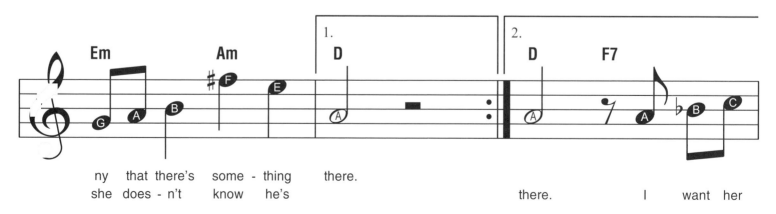

ny that there's some - thing there.

she does - n't know he's there. I want her

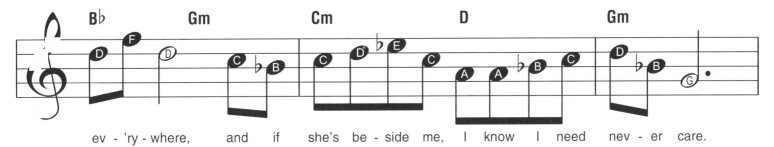

ev - 'ry - where,   and   if   she's   be - side   me,   I   know   I   need   nev - er   care.

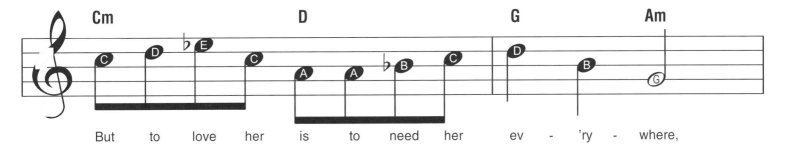

But   to   love   her   is   to   need   her   ev - 'ry - where,

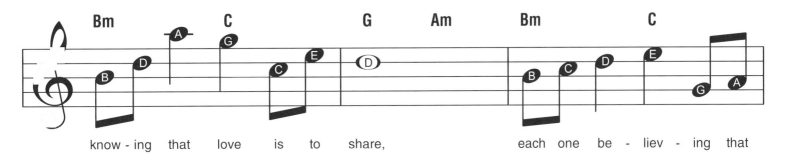

know - ing   that   love   is   to   share,   each   one   be - liev - ing   that

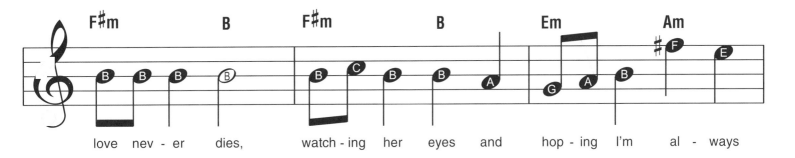

love   nev - er   dies,   watch - ing   her   eyes   and   hop - ing   I'm   al - ways

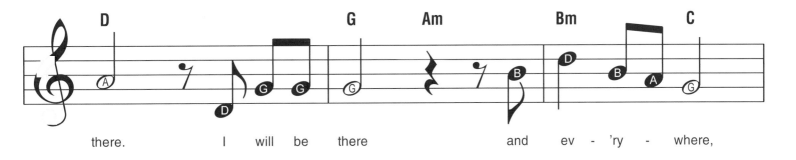

there.   I   will   be   there   and   ev - 'ry - where,

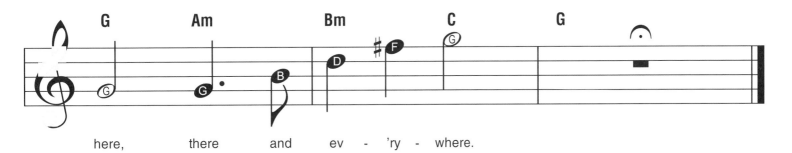

here,   there   and   ev - 'ry - where.

I Can't Make You Love Me

Words and Music by Mike Reid
and Allen Shamblin

Moderately slow

Turn down the lights, turn down the bed, turn down these voic - es

in - side my head. Lay down with me, tell me no lies.

Just hold me close, don't pa - tron - ize, _____ don't pa - tron -

ize _____ me. 'Cause I can't make you love me if you

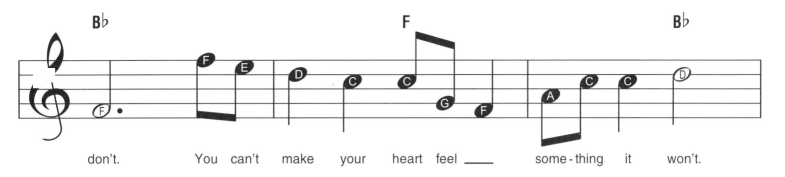

don't. You can't make your heart feel ____ some-thing it won't.

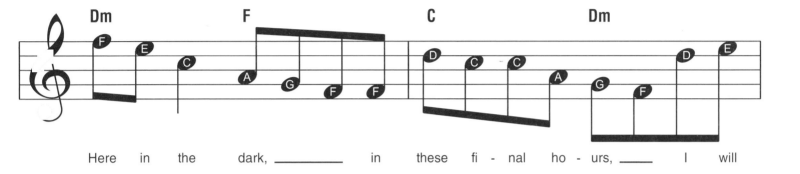

Here in the dark, _____ in these fi - nal ho - urs, ____ I will

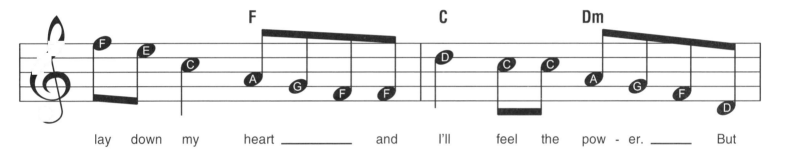

lay down my heart _____ and I'll feel the pow - er. _____ But

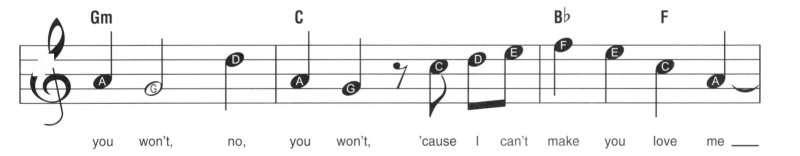

you won't, no, you won't, 'cause I can't make you love me ____

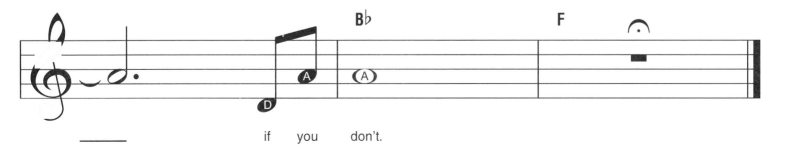

_____ if you don't.

I Get to Love You

Words and Music by Maggie Eckford
and Matt Bronleewe

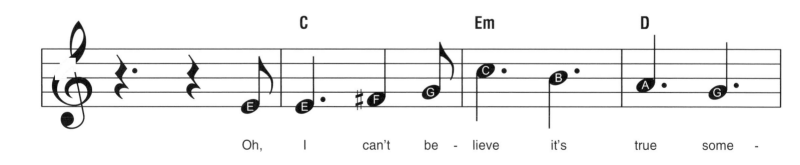

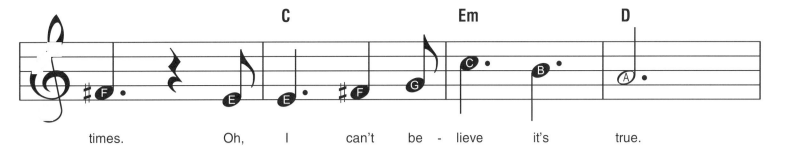

times.   Oh,   I   can't   be - lieve   it's   true.

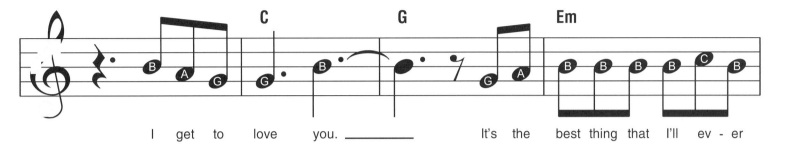

I   get   to   love   you. _____   It's   the   best thing that   I'll   ev - er

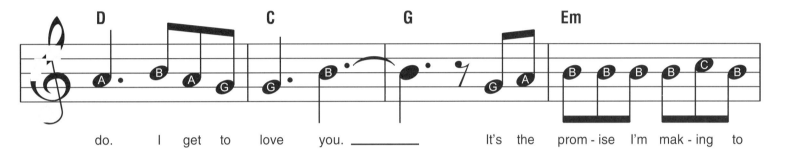

do.   I   get   to   love   you. _____   It's   the   prom - ise   I'm   mak - ing   to

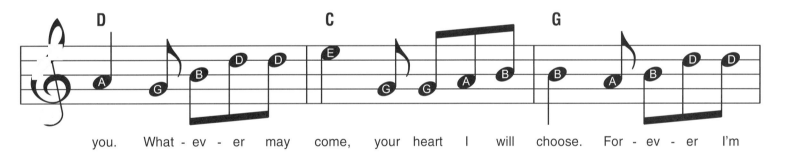

you.   What - ev - er   may   come,   your   heart   I   will   choose.   For - ev - er   I'm

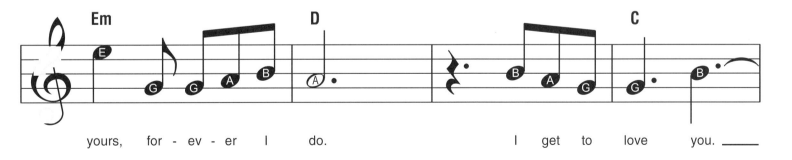

yours,   for - ev - er   I   do.   I   get   to   love   you. _____

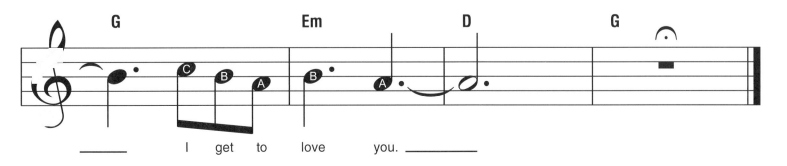

_____   I   get   to   love   you. _____

I Only Have Eyes for You

from DAMES

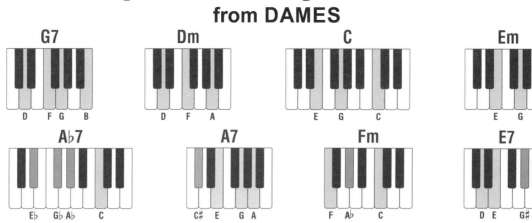

Words by Al Dubin
Music by Harry Warren

Moderately

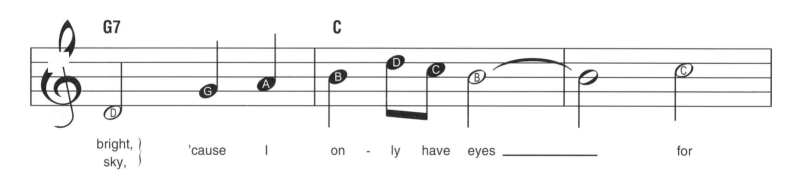

Are the stars out to - night? I don't know if it's cloud - y or
moon may be high, but I know can't see a thing in the

bright,
sky, } 'cause I on - ly have eyes _____ for

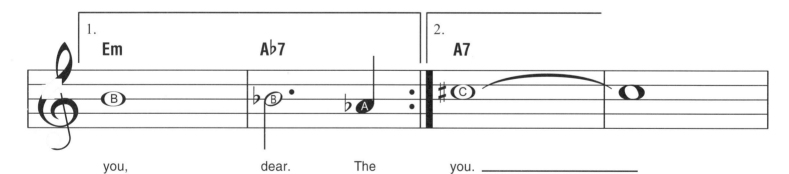

1.
you, dear. The

2.
you. _____

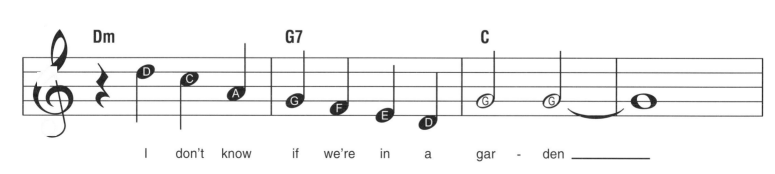

I don't know if we're in a gar - den _____

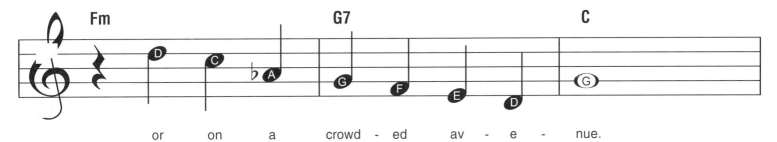

or on a crowd - ed av - e - nue.

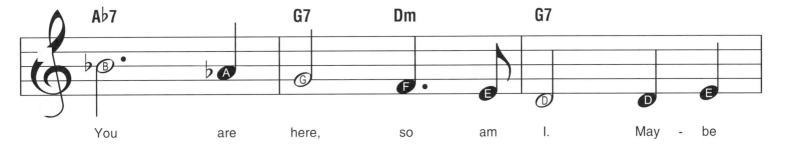

You are here, so am I. May - be

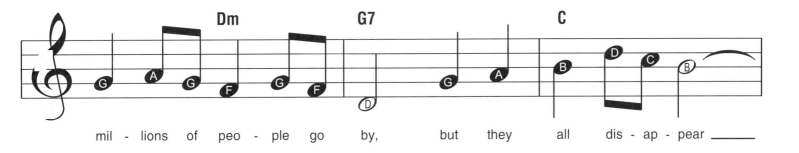

mil - lions of peo - ple go by, but they all dis - ap - pear _____

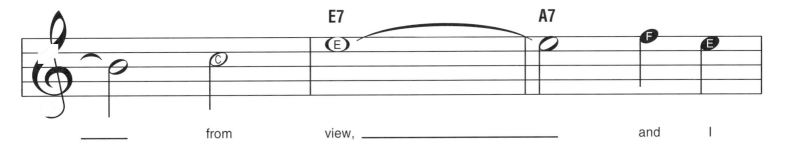

_____ from view, _____ and I

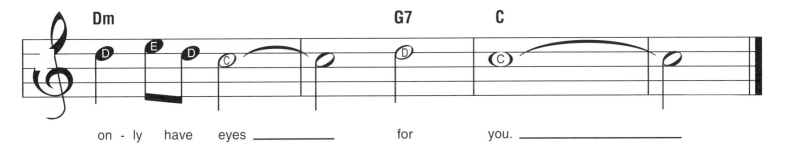

on - ly have eyes _____ for you. _____

I'll Be Seeing You

from RIGHT THIS WAY

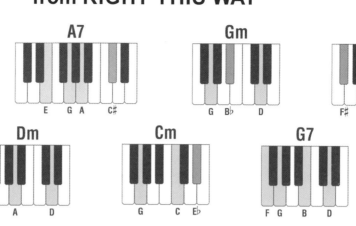

Written by Irving Kahal
and Sammy Fain

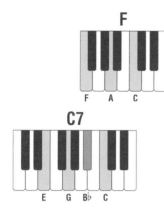

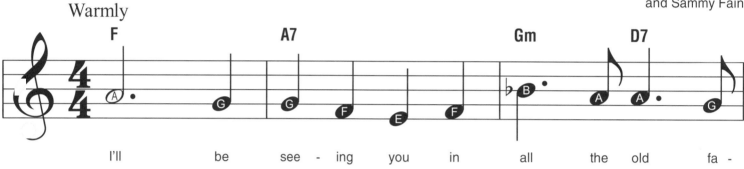

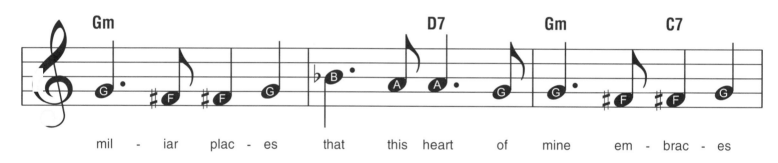

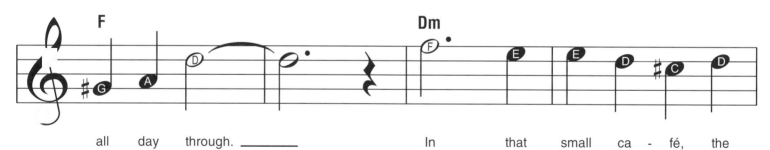

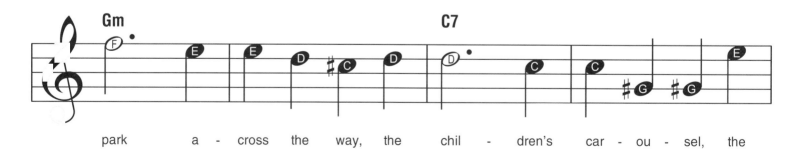

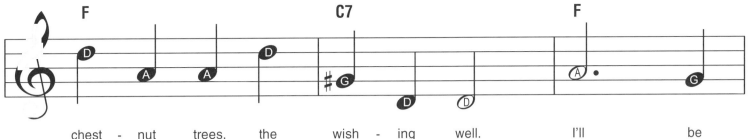

chest - nut trees, the wish - ing well. I'll be

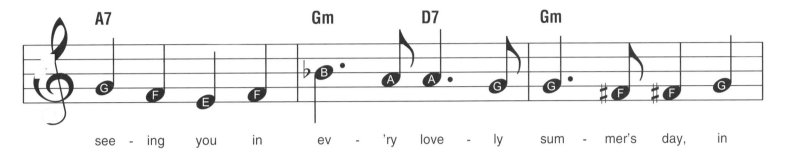

see - ing you in ev - 'ry love - ly sum - mer's day, in

ev - 'ry - thing that's light and gay. I'll al - ways think of

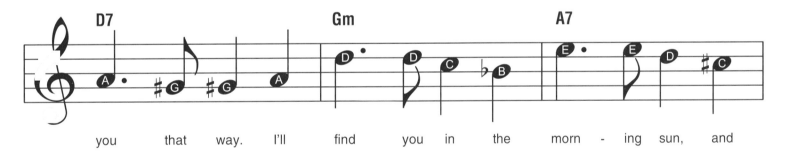

you that way. I'll find you in the morn - ing sun, and

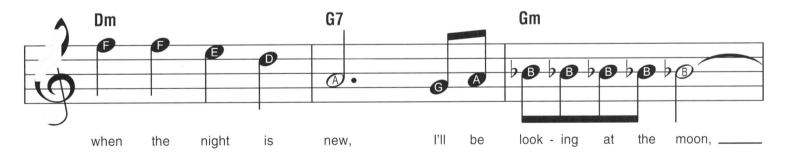

when the night is new, I'll be look - ing at the moon, _____

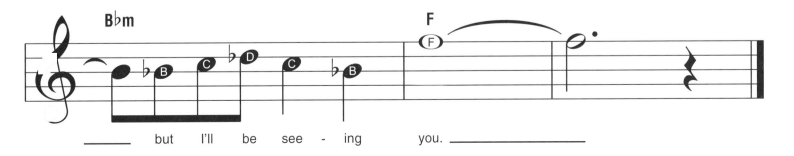

_____ but I'll be see - ing you. _____

I'll Never Love Again
from A STAR IS BORN

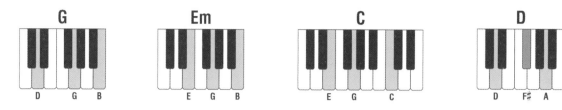

Words and Music by Stefani Germanotta,
Aaron Raitiere, Hillary Lindsey
and Natalie Hemby

With emotion
(no chord)

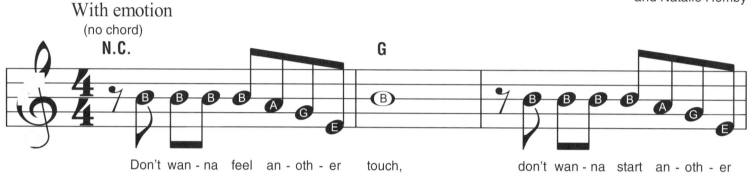

Don't wan-na feel an-oth-er touch, don't wan-na start an-oth-er

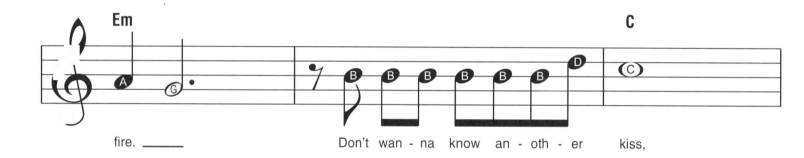

fire. _____ Don't wan-na know an-oth-er kiss,

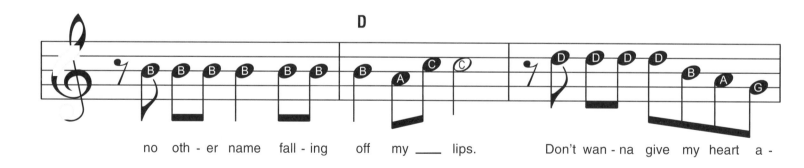

no oth-er name fall-ing off my ___ lips. Don't wan-na give my heart a-

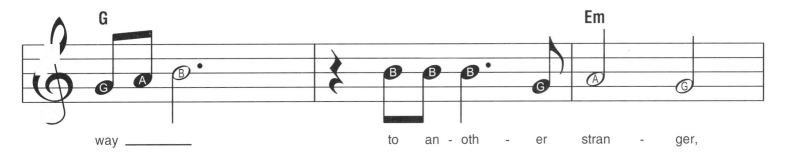

way _____ to an - oth - er stran - ger,

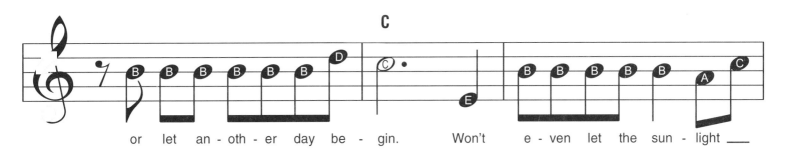

or let an - oth - er day be - gin. Won't e - ven let the sun - light ___

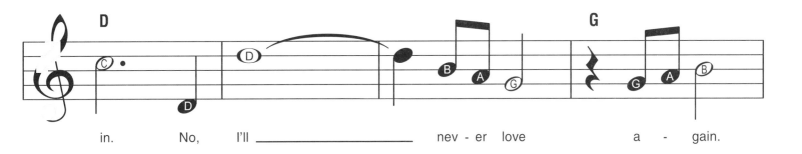

in. No, I'll _____ nev - er love a - gain.

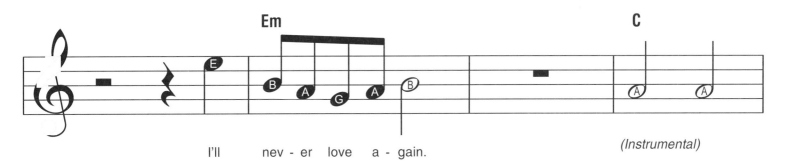

I'll nev - er love a - gain.   (Instrumental)

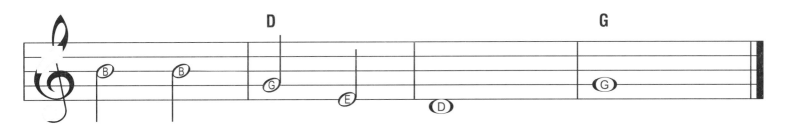

If Ever I Would Leave You

from CAMELOT

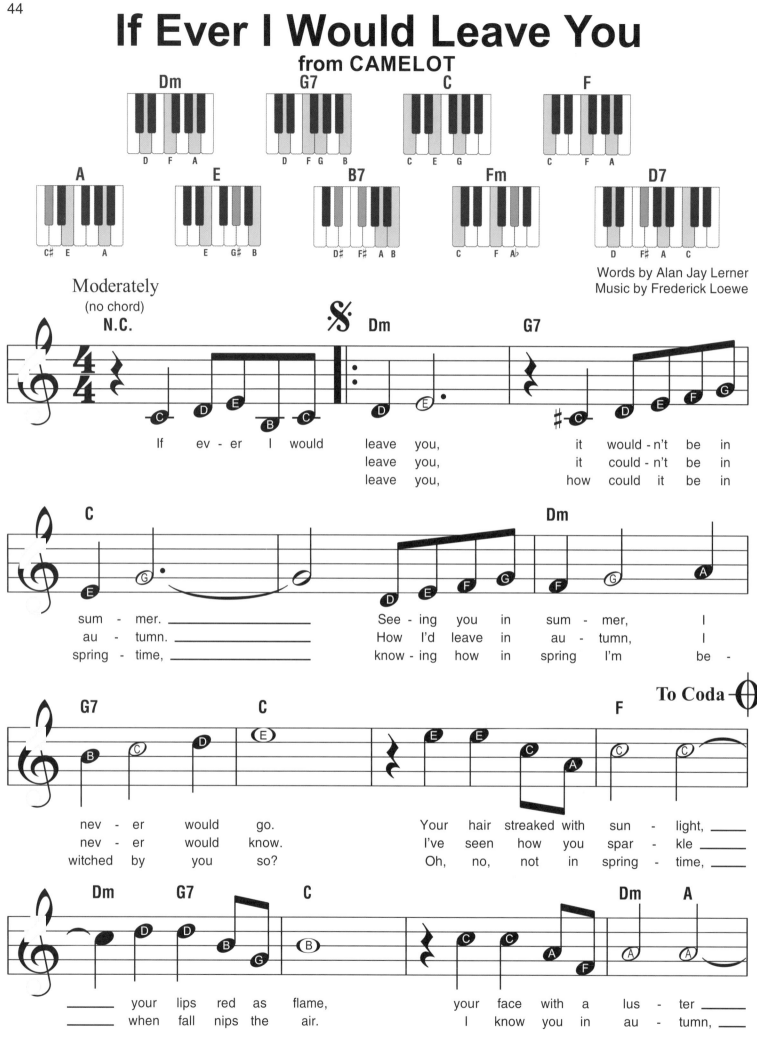

Words by Alan Jay Lerner
Music by Frederick Loewe

If You Don't Know Me by Now

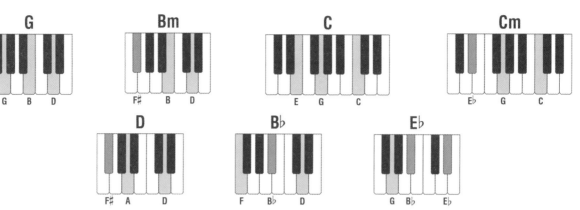

Words and Music by Kenneth Gamble
and Leon Huff

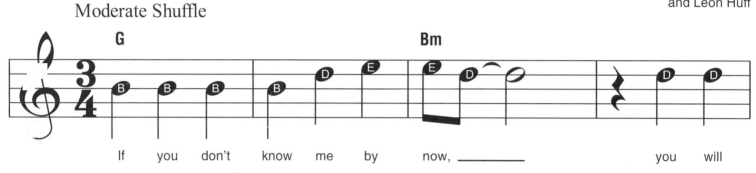

Moderate Shuffle

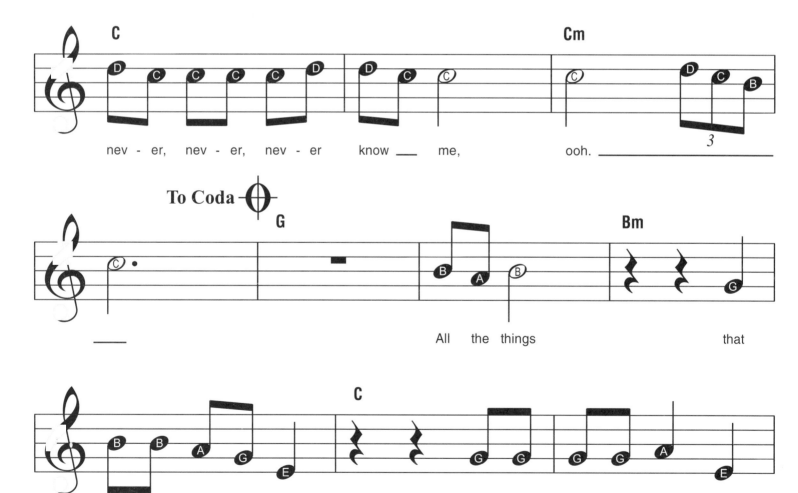

If you don't know me by now, _____ you will nev-er, nev-er, nev-er know ___ me, ooh. _____

All the things that we've been through, _____ you should un-der-stand me

In My Life

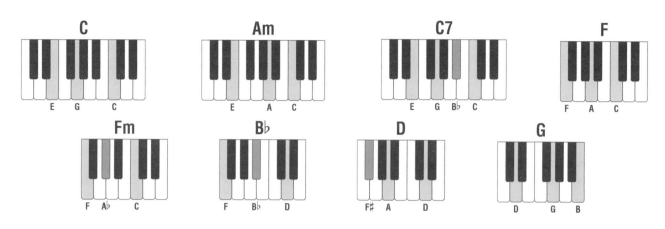

Words and Music by John Lennon
and Paul McCartney

Moderately

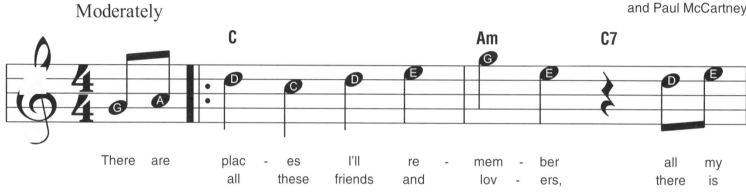

There are plac - es I'll re - mem - ber, all my
all these friends and lov - ers, there is

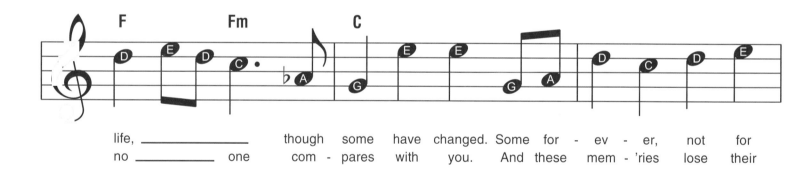

life, _____ though some have changed. Some for - ev - er, not for
no _____ one com - pares with you. And these mem - 'ries lose their

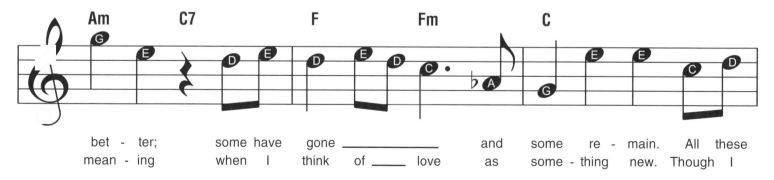

bet - ter; some have gone _____ and some re - main. All these
mean - ing when I think of ____ love as some - thing new. Though I

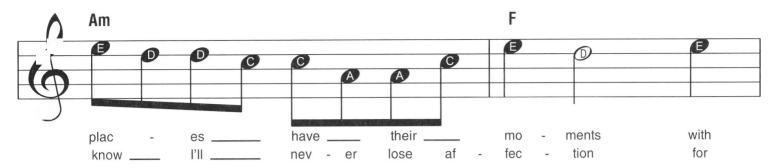

plac - es _____ have _____ their _____ mo - ments with
know _____ I'll _____ nev - er lose af - fec - tion for

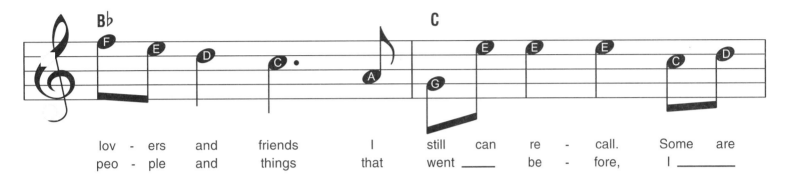

lov - ers and friends I still can re - call. Some are
peo - ple and things that went _____ be - fore, I _____

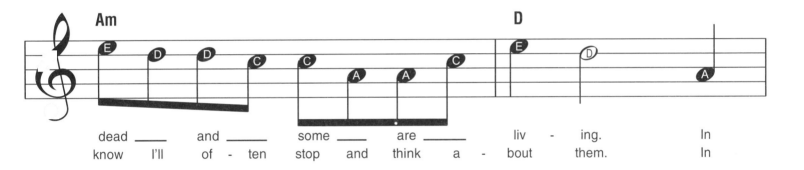

dead _____ and _____ some _____ are _____ liv - ing. In
know I'll of - ten stop and think a - bout them. In

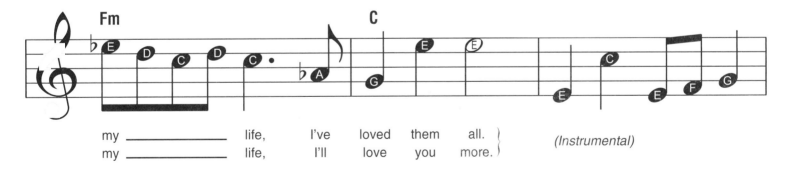

my _____ life, I've loved them all. ⎫
my _____ life, I'll love you more. ⎬   *(Instrumental)*

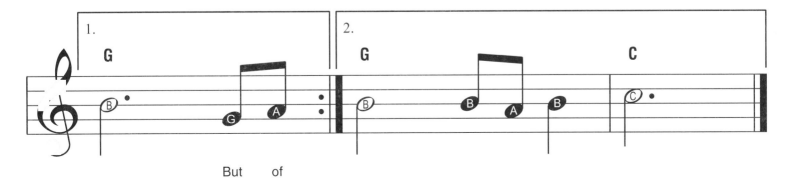

But of

It Must Have Been Love
featured in the Motion Picture PRETTY WOMAN

Words and Music by
Per Gessle

It must have been love, but it's o-ver now. _____ It must have been
It must have been love, but it's o-ver now. _____ It was all that I

good, but I lost it some-how. It must have been love, but it's o-ver
want-ed; now I'm liv-ing with-out. It must have been love, but it's o-ver

1. now, _____ from the mo-ment we touched till the time had run out. Make be-

2. now. It's where the wa-ter flows. _____ It's where the

wind ___ blows. _____

Kiss from a Rose

featured in the Motion Picture BATMAN FOREVER

Words and Music by
Henry Olusegun Adeola Samuel

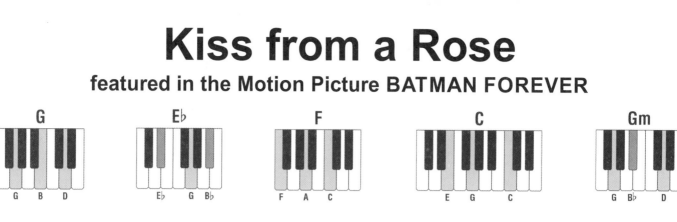

There _____ used to be a gray-ing tow - er a -
lone on the sea. _____ You _____ be - came the
light on the dark side of me. _____ Love _____ re -
mained a drug that's the high and not the pill. _____
But did you know that when it snows, my eyes be - come

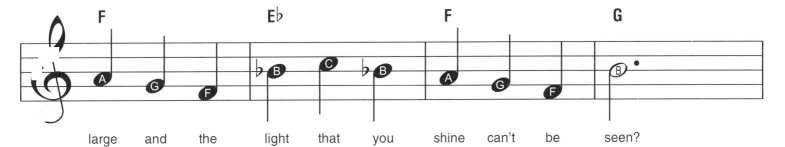

large and the light that you shine can't be seen?

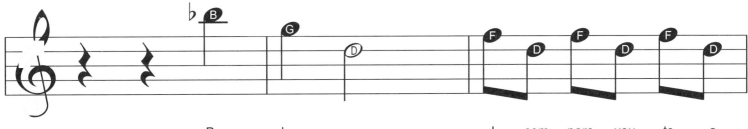

Ba - by, _____ I com - pare you to a

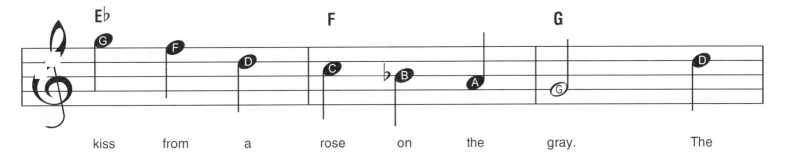

kiss from a rose on the gray. The

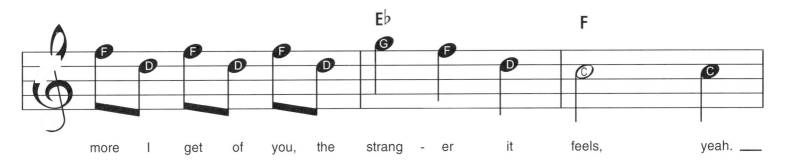

more I get of you, the strang - er it feels, yeah. ___

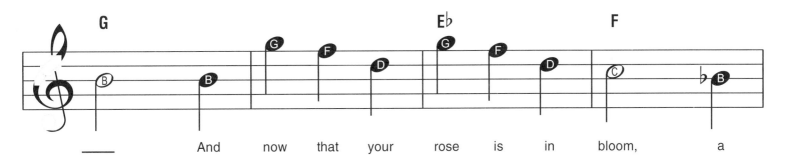

___ And now that your rose is in bloom, a

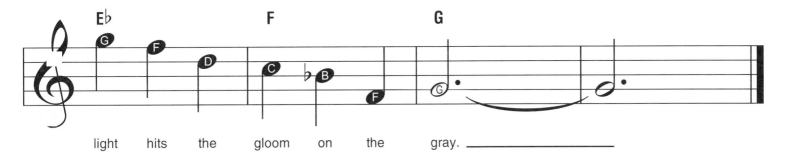

light hits the gloom on the gray. _____

The Long and Winding Road

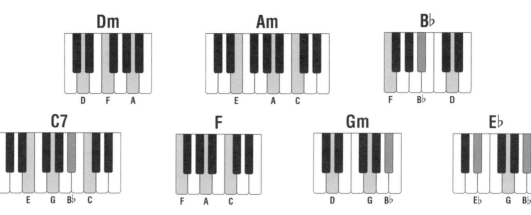

Words and Music by John Lennon
and Paul McCartney

Moderately slow

The long and wind-ing road that _____ leads to your
wild and wind-y night that the leads rain to washed a-

door will nev-er dis-ap-pear.
way has left a pool of tears

I've seen that road be-fore. _____ It al-ways
cry-ing for the day. _____ Why leave me

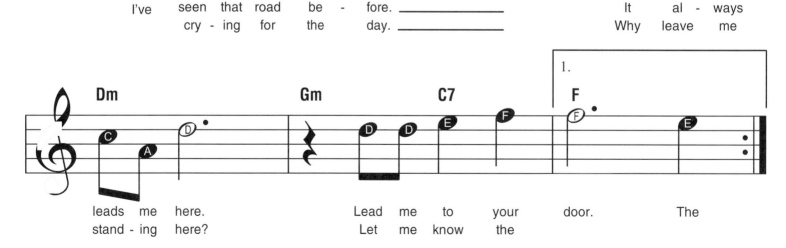

leads me here. Lead me to your door. The
stand-ing here? Let me know the

Love of My Life

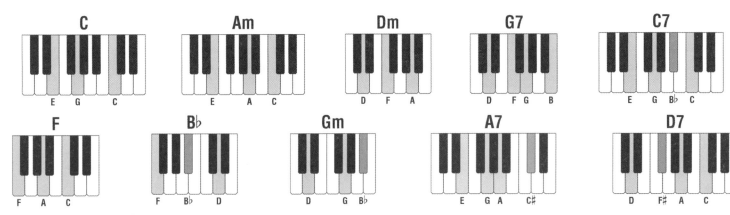

Words and Music by
Freddie Mercury

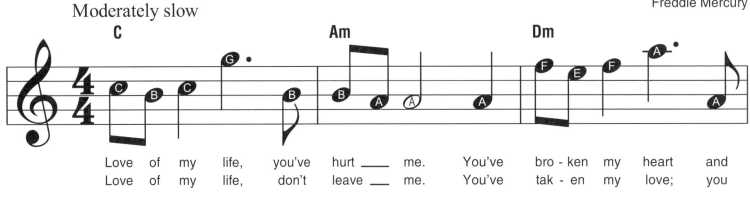

Love of my life, you've hurt ___ me. You've bro - ken my heart and
Love of my life, don't leave ___ me. You've tak - en my love; you

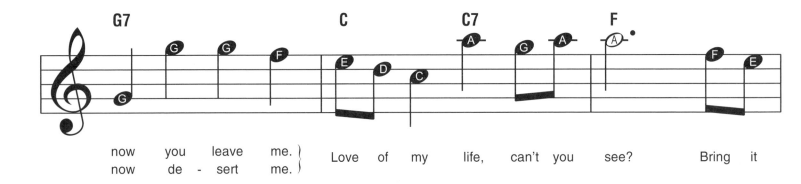

now you leave me. } Love of my life, can't you see? Bring it
now de - sert me. }

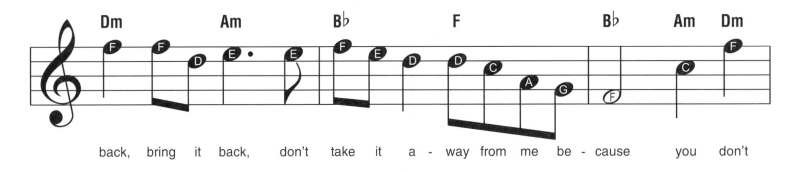

back, bring it back, don't take it a - way from me be - cause you don't

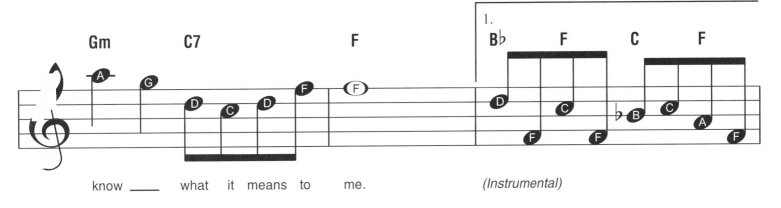

know _____ what it means to me. *(Instrumental)*

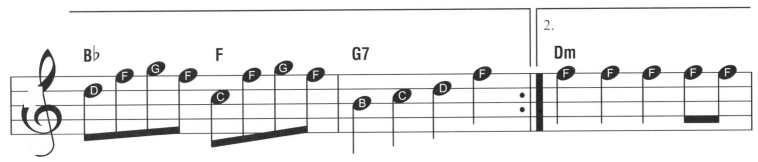

You'll re - mem - ber when

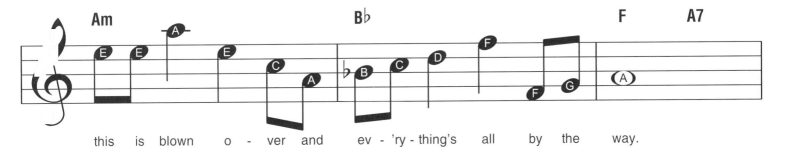

this is blown o - ver and ev - 'ry - thing's all by the way.

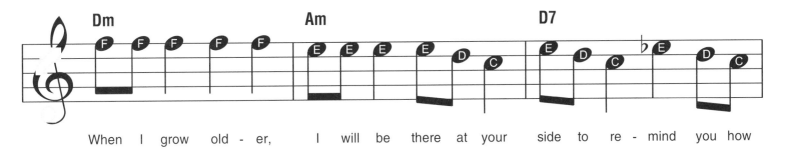

When I grow old - er, I will be there at your side to re - mind you how

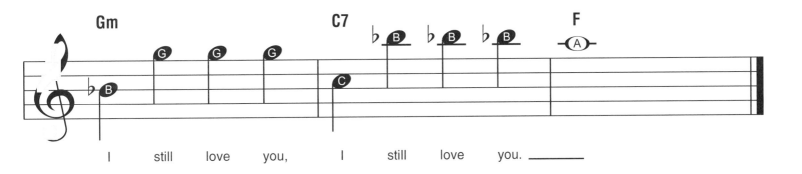

I still love you, I still love you. _____

My Way

English Words by Paul Anka
Original French Words by Gilles Thibault
Music by Jacques Revaux and Claude François

The Nearness of You
from the Paramount Picture ROMANCE IN THE DARK

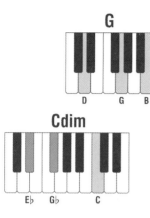
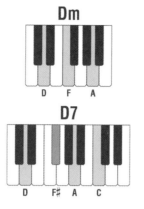
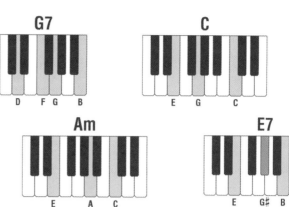

Words by Ned Washington
Music by Hoagy Carmichael

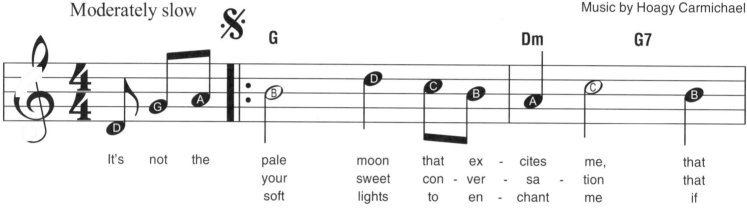

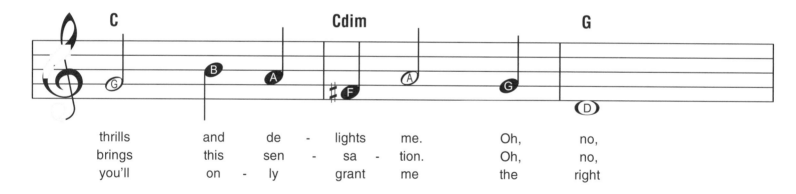

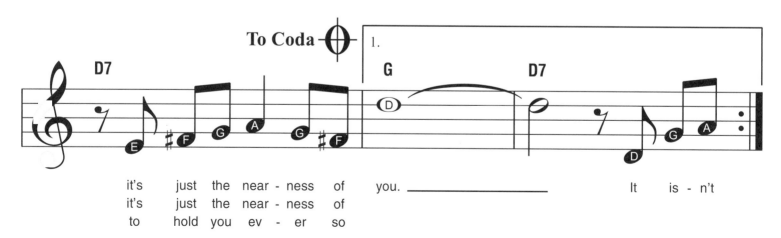

you. _____ When you're in my arms _____

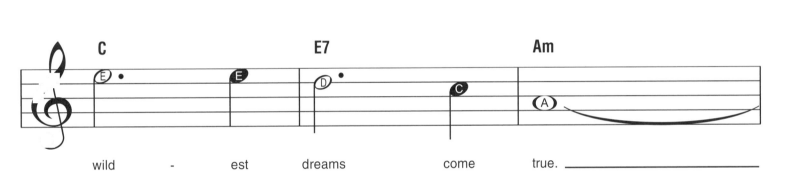

_____ and I feel you so close to me, _____ all my

wild - est dreams come true. _____

D.S. al Coda
(Return to 𝄋, play to ⊕
and skip to Coda)

CODA

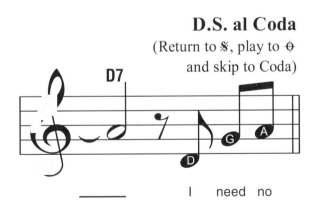

_____ I need no

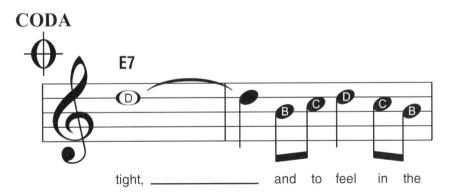

tight, _____ and to feel in the

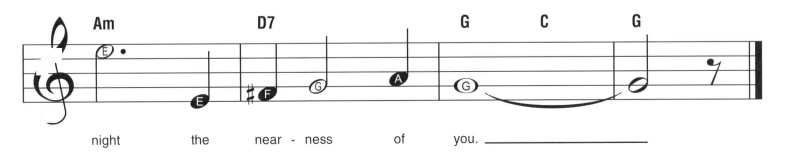

night the near - ness of you. _____

Never Enough
from THE GREATEST SHOWMAN

Words and Music by Benj Pasek
and Justin Paul

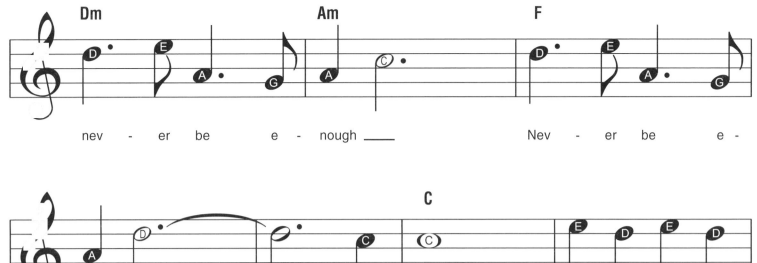

nev - er be e - nough _____ Nev - er be e -

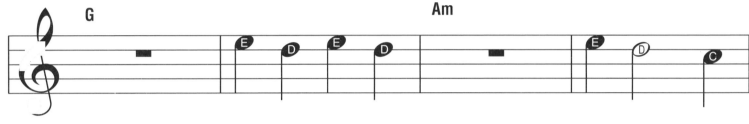

nough _____ for me Nev - er, nev - er

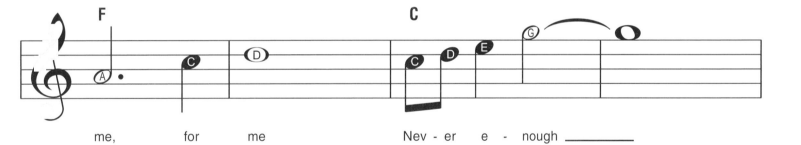

Nev - er, nev - er Nev - er for

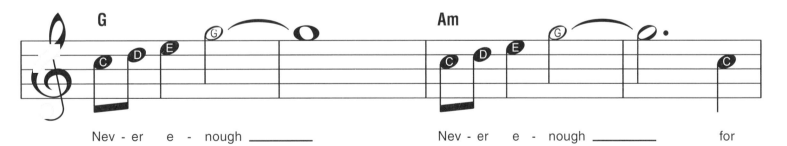

me, for me Nev - er e - nough _____

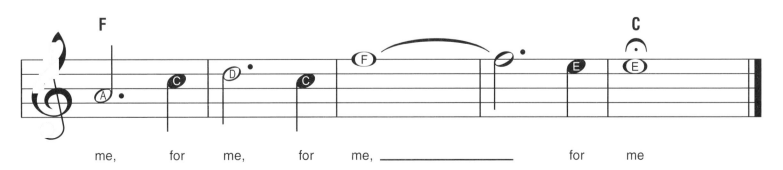

Nev - er e - nough _____ Nev - er e - nough _____ for

me, for me, for me, _____ for me

On My Own
from LES MISÉRABLES

Music by Claude-Michel Schönberg
Lyrics by Alain Boublil,
Jean-Marc Natel, Herbert Kretzmer,
John Caird and Trevor Nunn

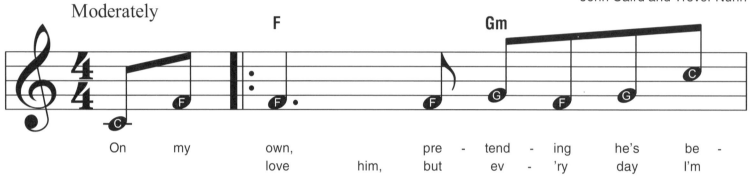

On my own, pre - tend - ing he's be -
love him, but ev - 'ry day I'm

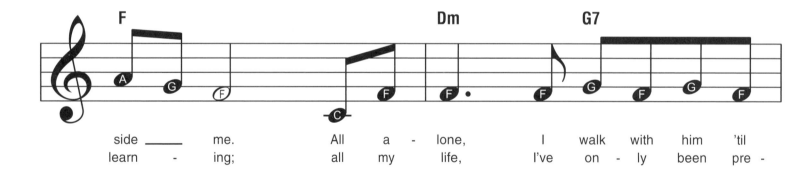

side _____ me. All a - lone, I walk with him 'til
learn - ing; all my life, I've on - ly been pre -

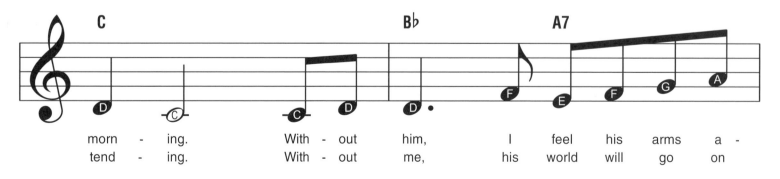

morn - ing. With - out him, I feel his arms a -
tend - ing. With - out me, his world will go on

round   me,   and   when   I   lose   my   way,   I   close   my
turn - ing.   The   world   is   full   of   hap - pi - ness   that

1.

eyes   and   he   has   found   me. _____

2.

I   have   nev - er   known. _____

love   him,   I   love   him,   I

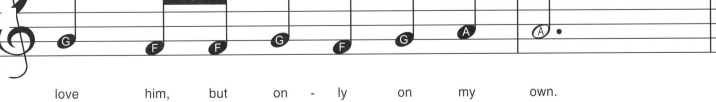

love   him,   but   on - ly   on   my   own.

People
from FUNNY GIRL

Words by Bob Merrill
Music by Jule Styne

Moderately, with expression

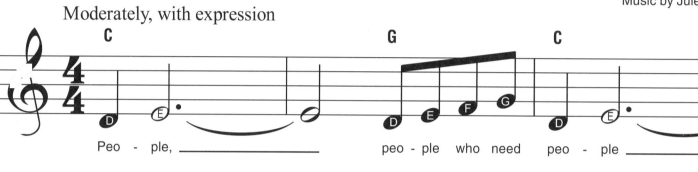

Peo - ple, _____ peo - ple who need peo - ple _____

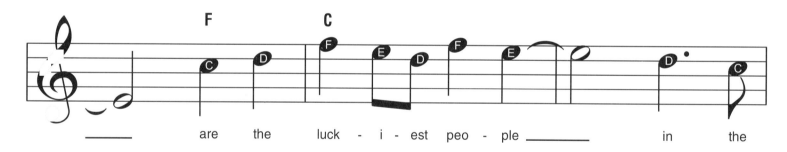

_____ are the luck - i - est peo - ple _____ in the

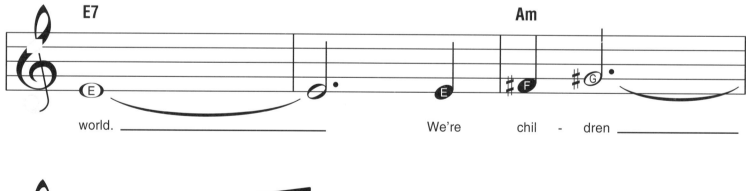

world. _____ We're chil - dren _____

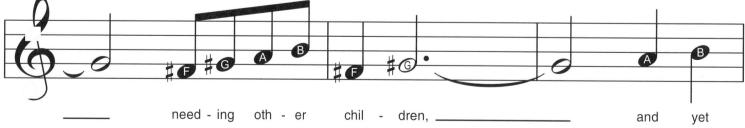

_____ need - ing oth - er chil - dren, _____ and yet

Right Here Waiting

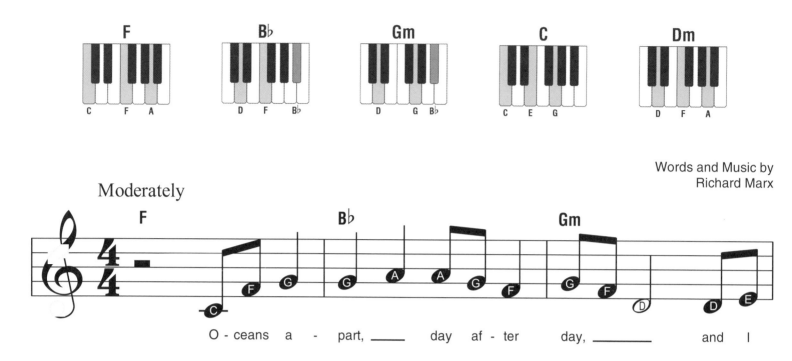

Words and Music by
Richard Marx

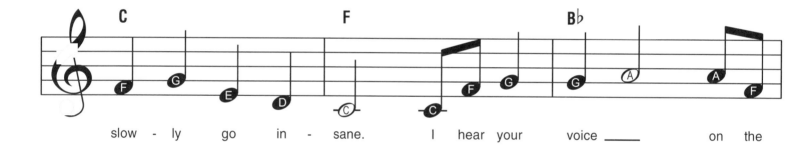

O - ceans a - part, _____ day af - ter day, _____ and I

slow - ly go in - sane. I hear your voice _____ on the

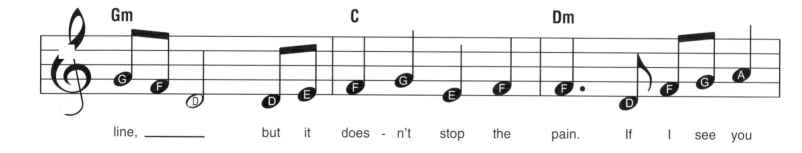

line, _____ but it does - n't stop the pain. If I see you

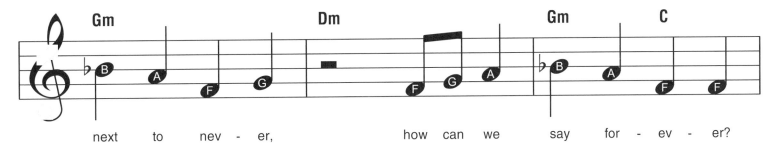

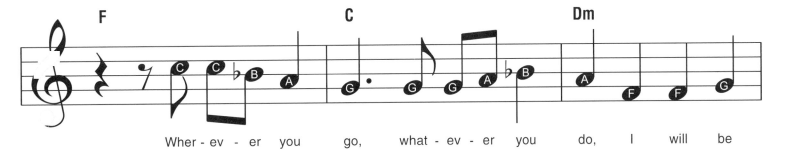

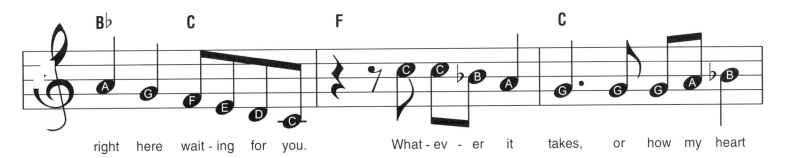

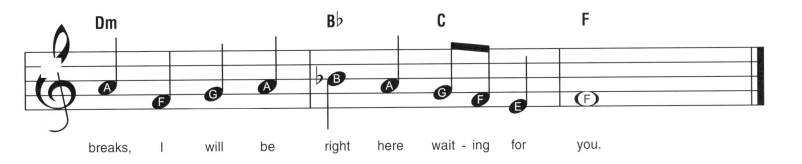

Rise Up

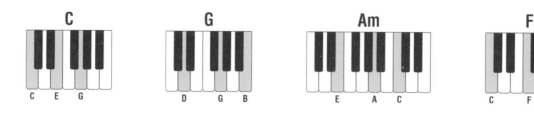

Words and Music by Cassandra Batie
and Jennifer Decilveo

Moderately slow

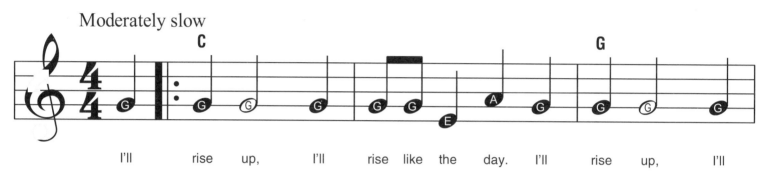

I'll rise up, I'll rise like the day. I'll rise up, I'll

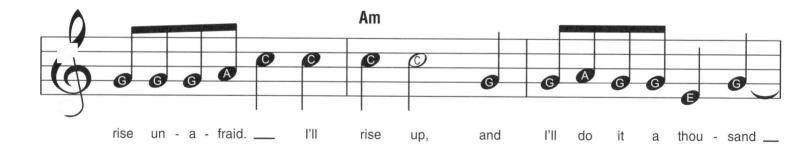

rise un - a - fraid. ___ I'll rise up, and I'll do it a thou - sand ___

_____ times a - gain. And I'll rise up, I'll

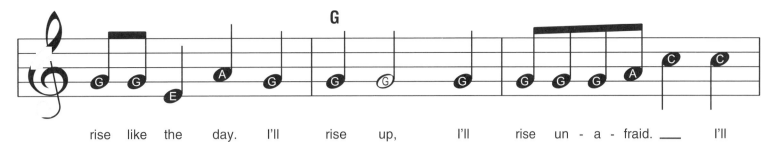

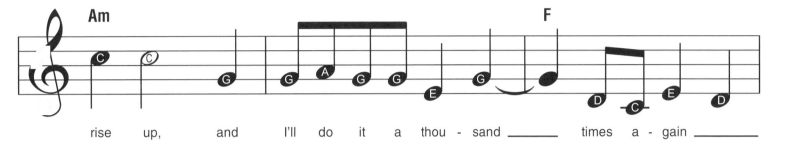

rise like the day. I'll rise up, I'll rise un - a - fraid. ___ I'll

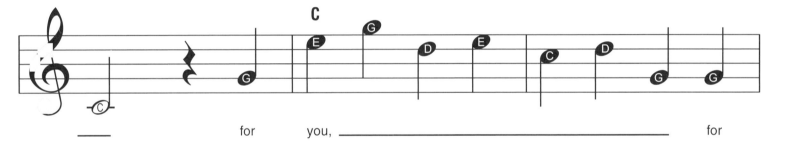

rise up, and I'll do it a thou - sand _____ times a - gain _____

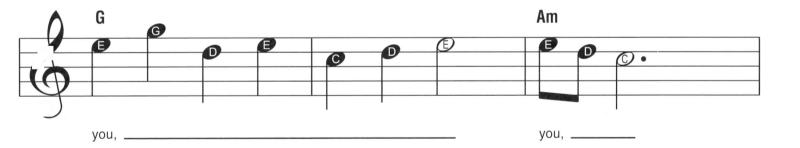

___ for you, _____ for

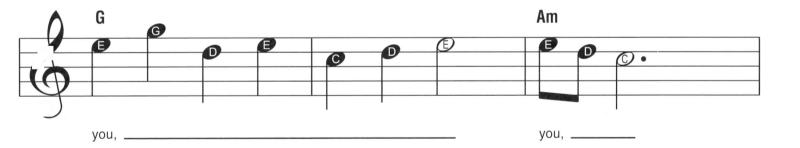

you, _____ you, _____

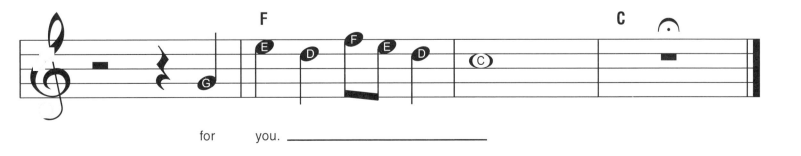

for you. _____

Some Enchanted Evening

from SOUTH PACIFIC

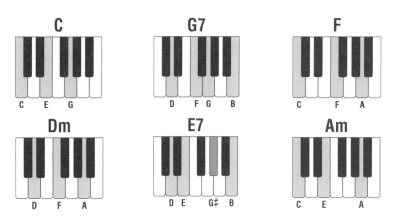

Lyrics by Oscar Hammerstein II
Music by Richard Rodgers

Moderately

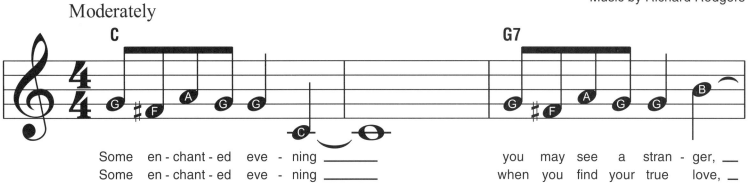

Some en-chant-ed eve-ning _____ you may see a stran-ger, __
Some en-chant-ed eve-ning _____ when you find your true love, __

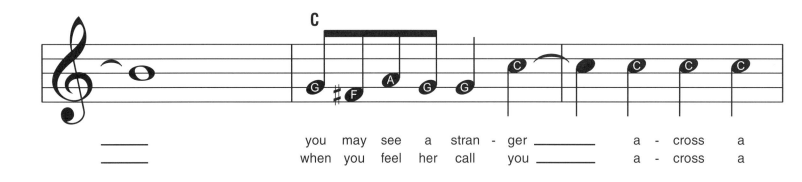

_____ you may see a stran-ger _____ a-cross a
_____ when you feel her call you _____ a-cross a

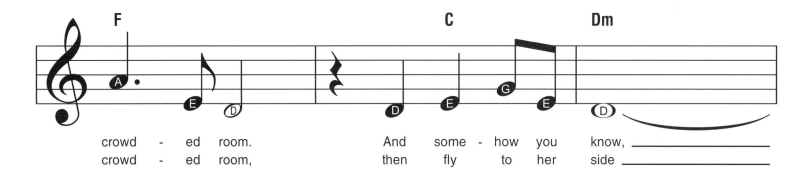

crowd-ed room. And some-how you know, _____
crowd-ed room, then fly to her side _____

Someone Like You

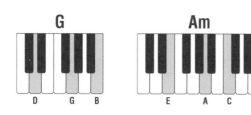
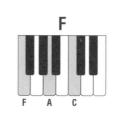
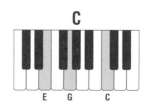

Words and Music by Adele Adkins
and Dan Wilson

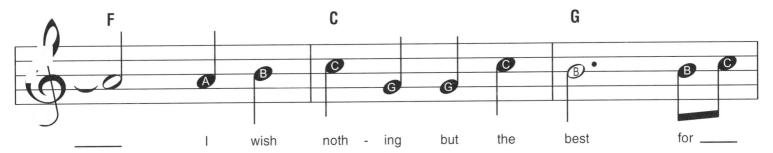

I wish noth - ing but the best for

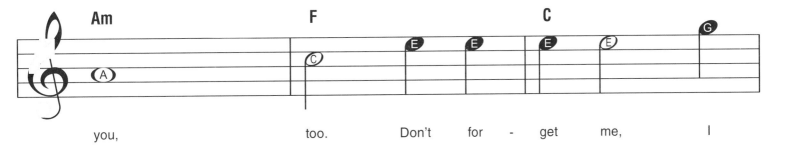

you, too. Don't for - get me, I

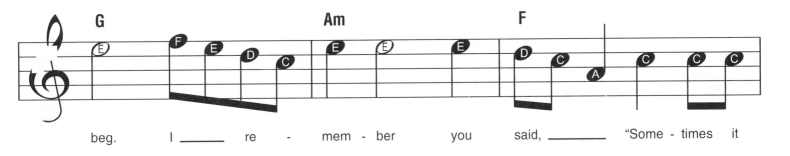

beg. I re - mem - ber you said, "Some - times it

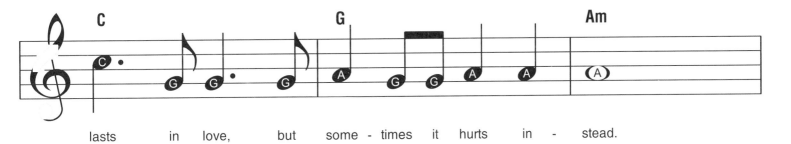

lasts in love, but some - times it hurts in - stead.

Some - times it lasts in love, but some - times it hurts in -

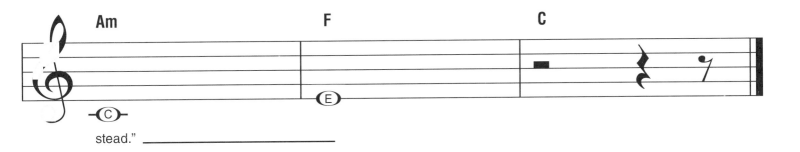

stead."

Someone You Loved

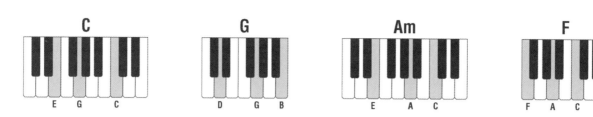

Words and Music by Lewis Capaldi,
Benjamin Kohn, Peter Kelleher,
Thomas Barnes and Samuel Roman

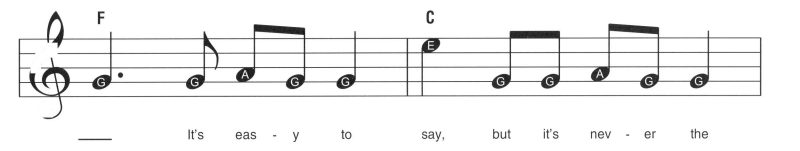

It's eas - y to say, but it's nev - er the

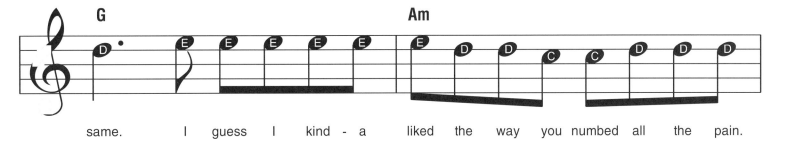

same. I guess I kind - a liked the way you numbed all the pain.

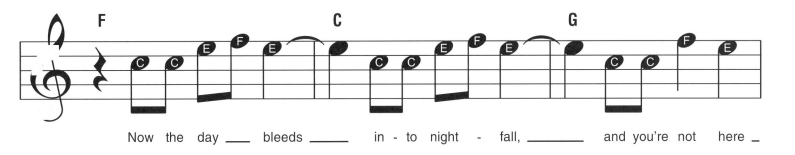

Now the day ___ bleeds ___ in - to night - fall, _____ and you're not here _

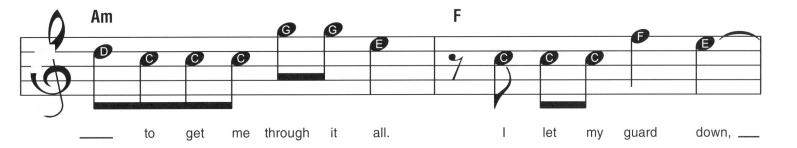

___ to get me through it all. I let my guard down, ___

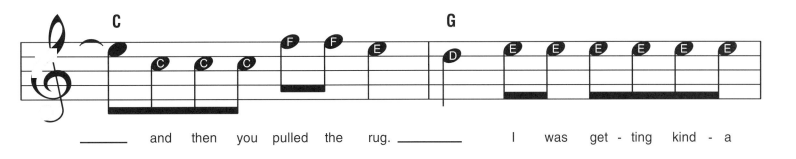

_____ and then you pulled the rug. _____ I was get - ting kind - a

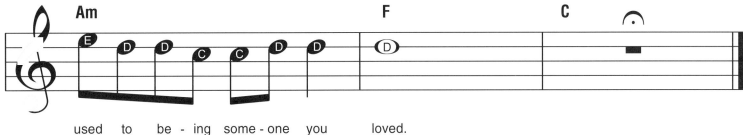

used to be - ing some - one you loved.

Sorry Seems to Be the Hardest Word

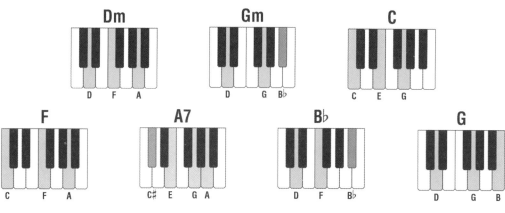

Words and Music by Elton John
and Bernie Taupin

Gentle Ballad

Dm / Gm

What-'ve I got to do to make you love me?
What do I _____ do to make you want me?

C

What-'ve I got to do _____ to make you
What-'ve I got to do _____ to be

F / Gm / A7 / Dm

care? What do I do when light-ning
heard? What do I say when it's all

1.

Gm

strikes me, and I wake to
o - ver,

C

and I wake to

Stay

Words and Music by Mikky Ekko
and Justin Parker

Stay with Me

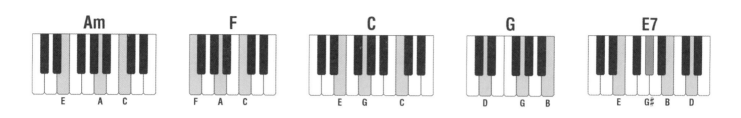

Words and Music by Sam Smith,
James Napier, William Edward Phillips,
Tom Petty and Jeff Lynne

Moderately slow

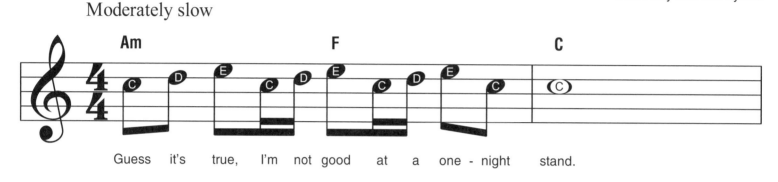

Guess it's true, I'm not good at a one - night stand.

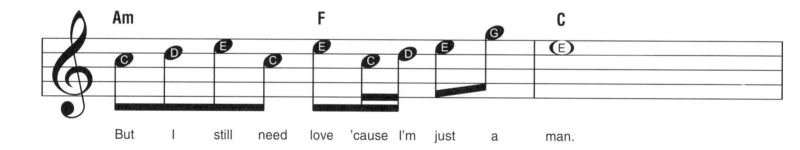

But I still need love 'cause I'm just a man.

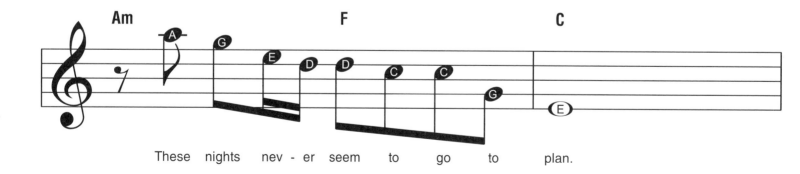

These nights nev - er seem to go to plan.

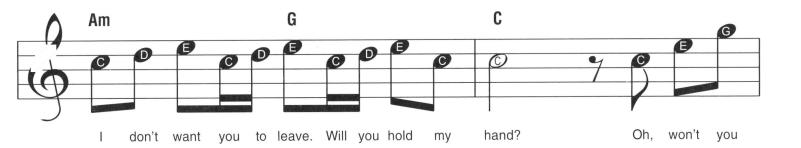

I don't want you to leave. Will you hold my hand? Oh, won't you

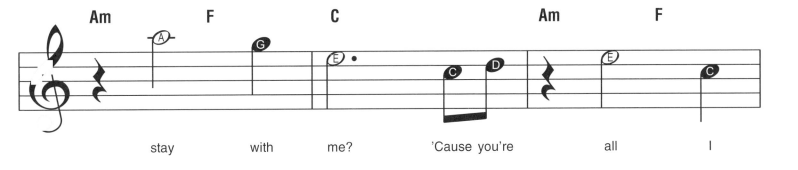

stay with me? 'Cause you're all I

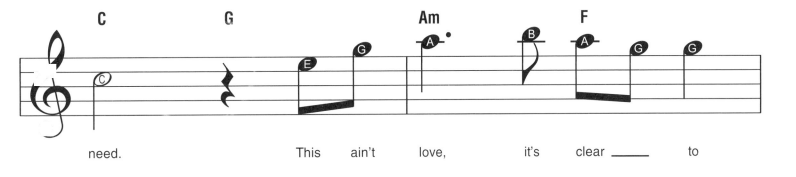

need. This ain't love, it's clear _____ to

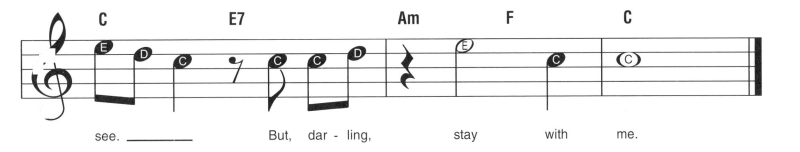

see. _____ But, dar - ling, stay with me.

Take My Breath Away
(Love Theme)
from the Paramount Picture TOP GUN

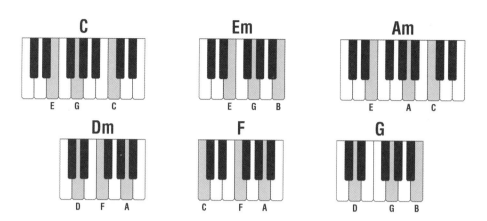

Words and Music by Giorgio Moroder
and Tom Whitlock

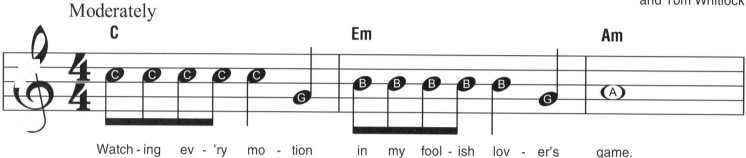

Watch-ing ev-'ry mo-tion in my fool-ish lov-er's game.

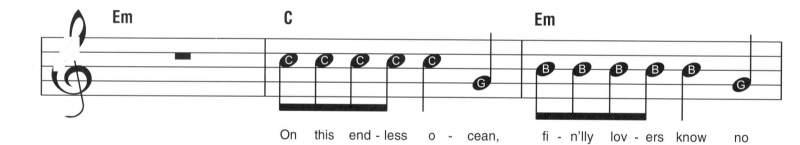

On this end-less o-cean, fi-n'lly lov-ers know no

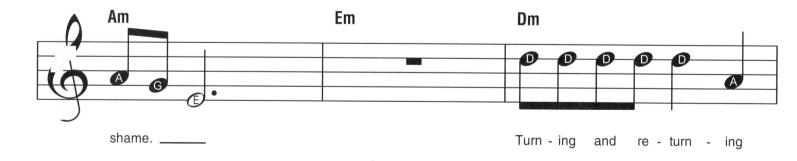

shame. _____ Turn-ing and re-turn-ing

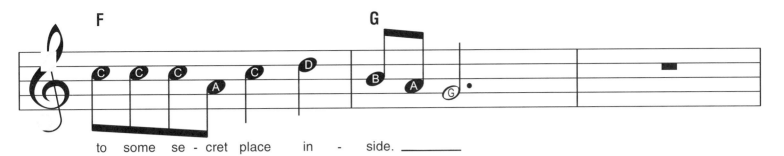

to some se - cret place in - side. _____

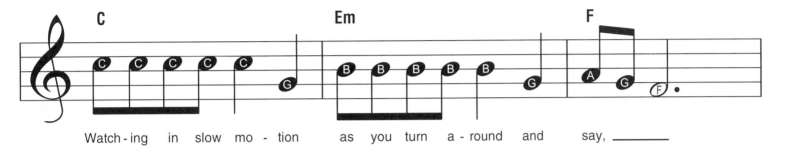

Watch - ing in slow mo - tion as you turn a - round and say, _____

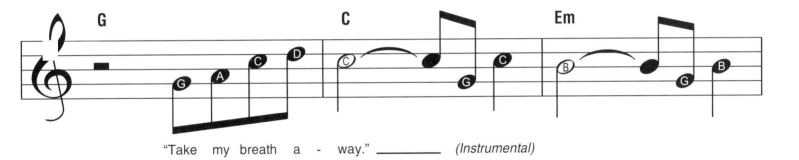

"Take my breath a - way." _____ (Instrumental)

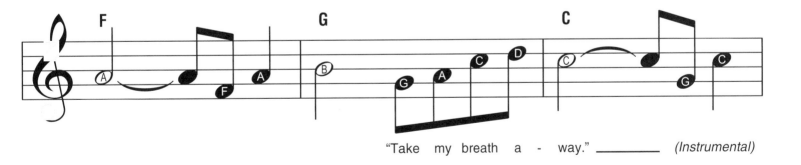

"Take my breath a - way." _____ (Instrumental)

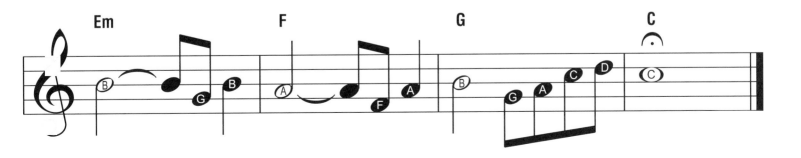

Tears in Heaven

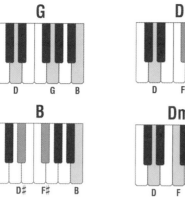
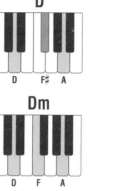
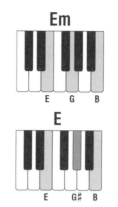
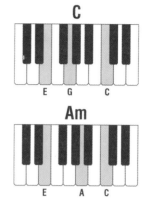

Words and Music by Eric Clapton
and Will Jennings

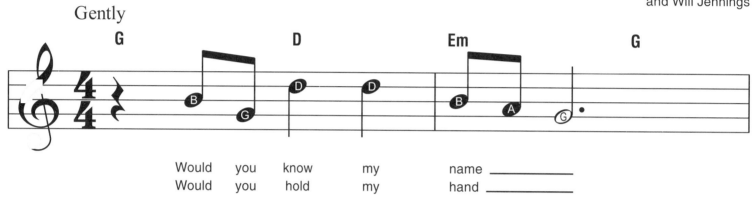

Would   you   know   my   name _____
Would   you   hold   my   hand _____

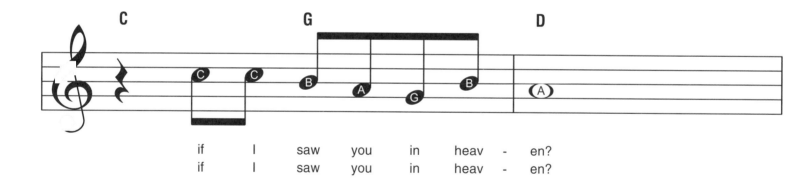

if   I   saw   you   in   heav - en?
if   I   saw   you   in   heav - en?

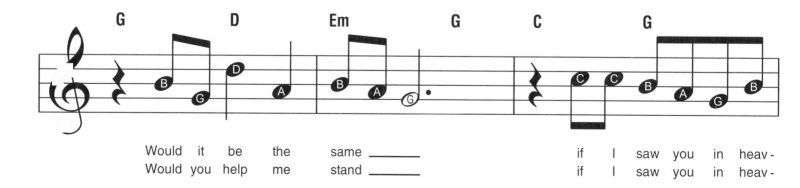

Would   it   be   the   same _____   if   I   saw   you   in   heav-
Would   you   help   me   stand _____   if   I   saw   you   in   heav-

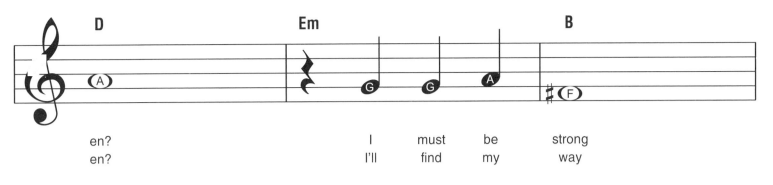

en?   I   must   be   strong
en?   I'll   find   my   way

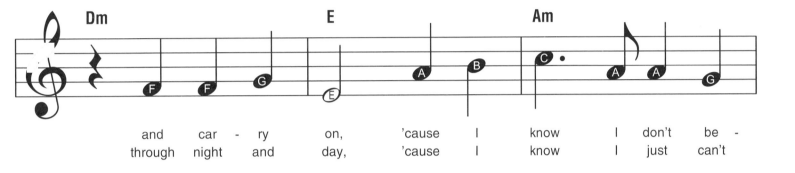

and   car - ry   on,   'cause   I   know   I   don't   be -
through   night   and   day,   'cause   I   know   I   just   can't

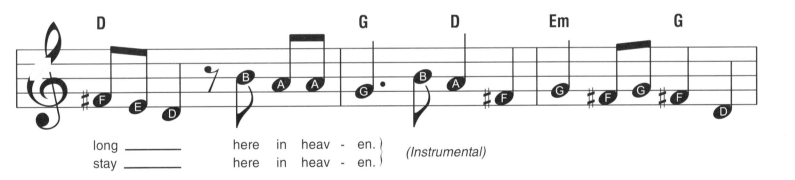

long _____ here   in   heav - en. }
stay _____ here   in   heav - en. } *(Instrumental)*

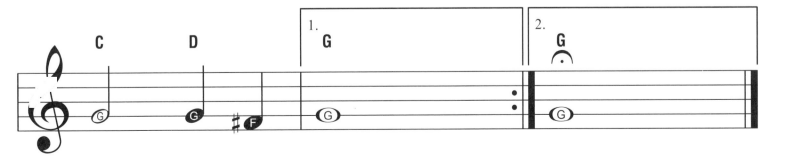

That's What Friends Are For

from NIGHT SHIFT

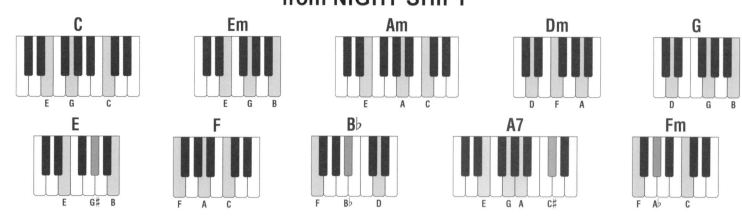

Music by Burt Bacharach
Words by Carole Bayer Sager

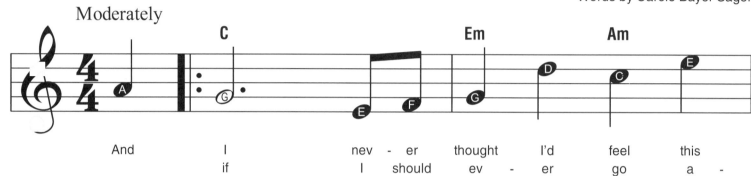

And I nev - er thought I'd feel this
if I should ev - er go a -

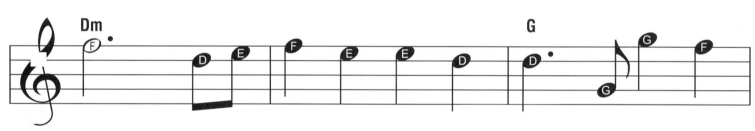

way, and as far as I'm con - cerned, I'm glad I
way, well, then close your eyes and try to feel the

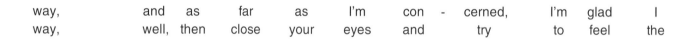

got the chance to say that I do be - lieve I
way we do to - day, and then if you can re -

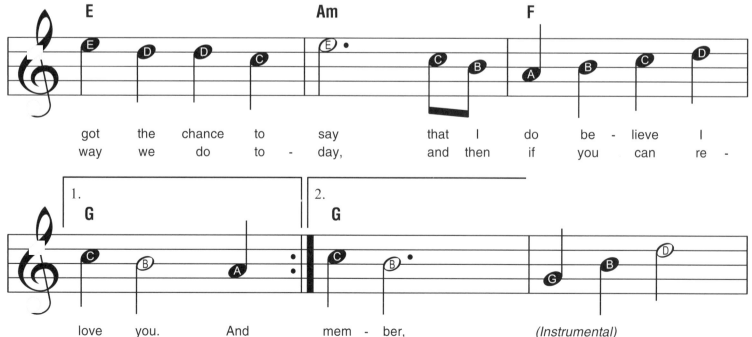

love you. And mem - ber, (Instrumental)

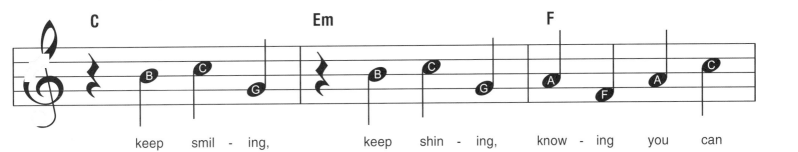

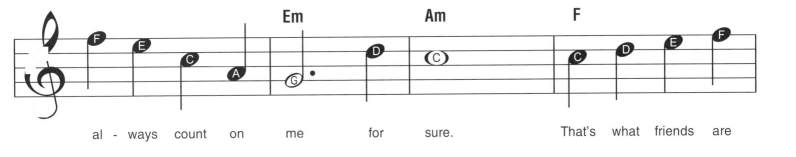

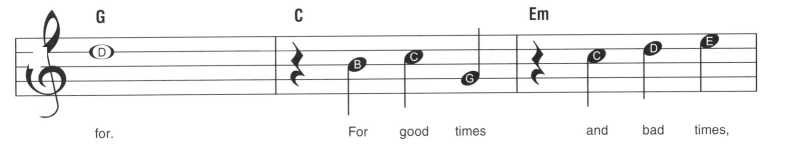

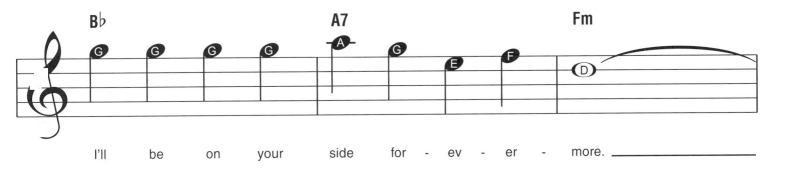

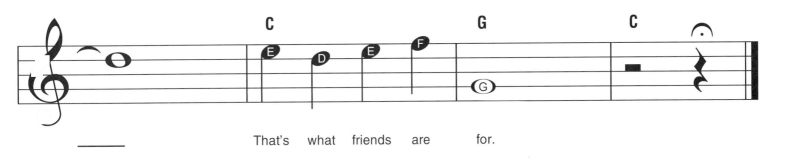

Through the Years

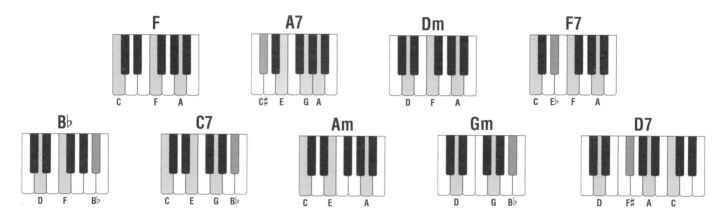

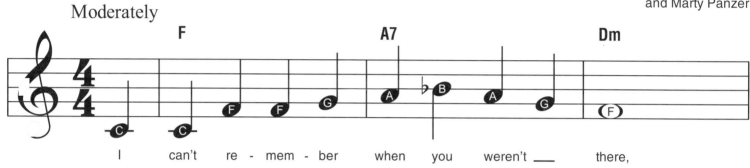

Words and Music by Steve Dorff
and Marty Panzer

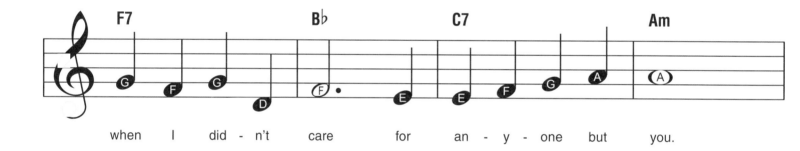

I can't re - mem - ber when you weren't ___ there,

when I did - n't care for an - y - one but you.

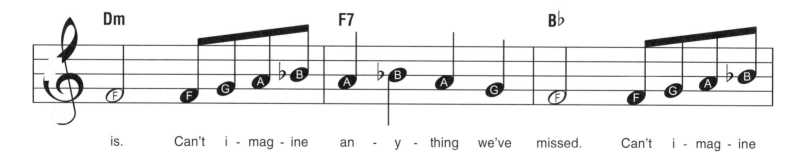

I swear _____ we've been through ev - 'ry - thing there

is. Can't i - mag - ine an - y - thing we've missed. Can't i - mag - ine

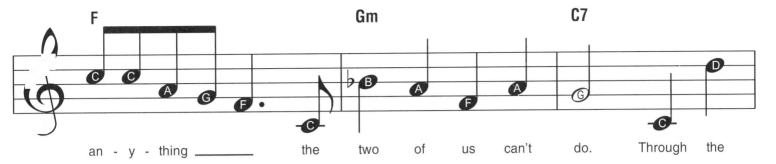

an - y - thing _____ the two of us can't do. Through the

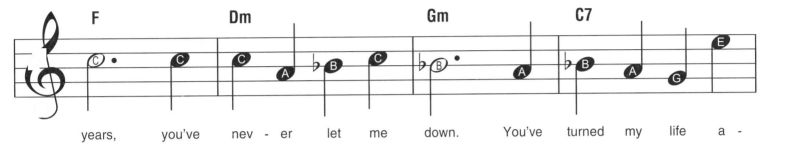

years, you've nev - er let me down. You've turned my life a -

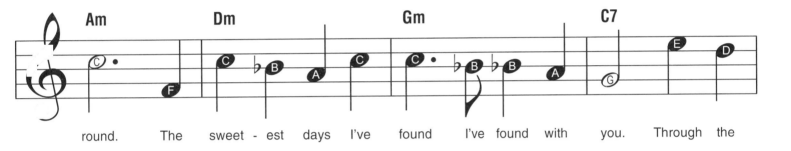

round. The sweet - est days I've found I've found with you. Through the

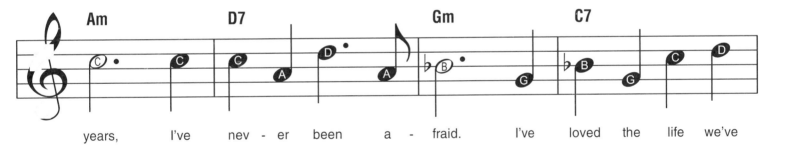

years, I've nev - er been a - fraid. I've loved the life we've

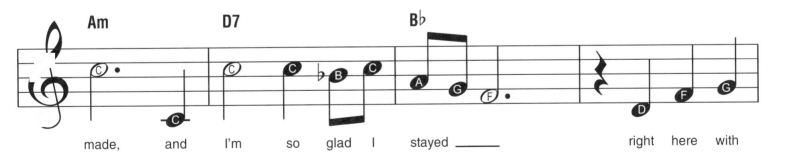

made, and I'm so glad I stayed _____ right here with

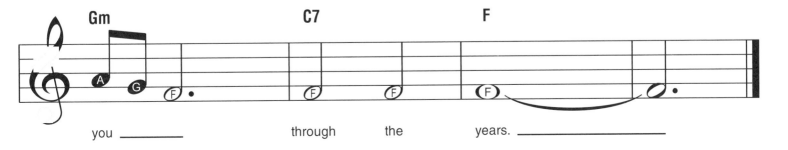

you _____ through the years. _____

Total Eclipse of the Heart

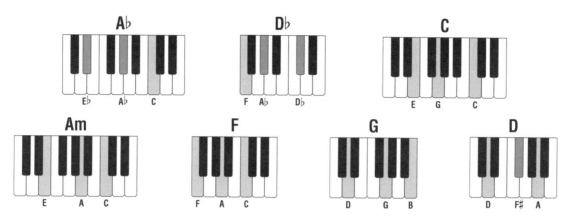

Words and Music by
Jim Steinman

Slow half-time feel

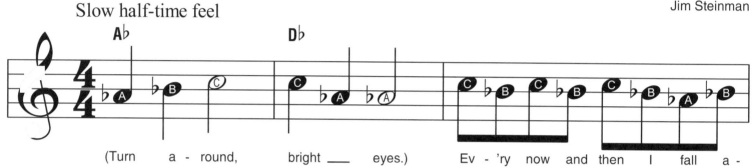

(Turn a - round, bright ___ eyes.) Ev - 'ry now and then I fall a -

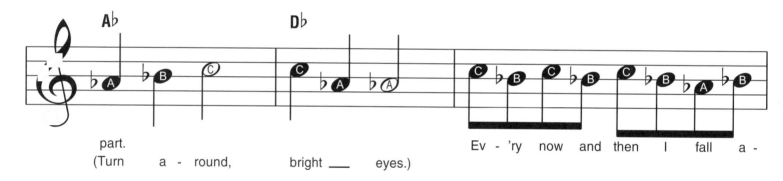

part.
(Turn a - round, bright ___ eyes.) Ev - 'ry now and then I fall a -

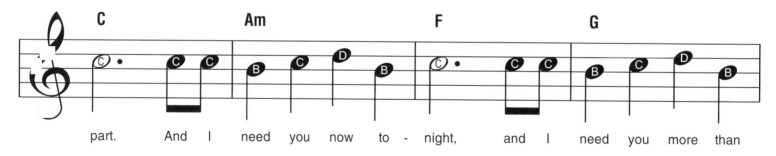

part. And I need you now to - night, and I need you more than

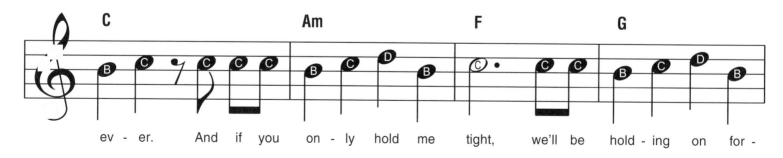

ev - er. And if you on - ly hold me tight, we'll be hold - ing on for -

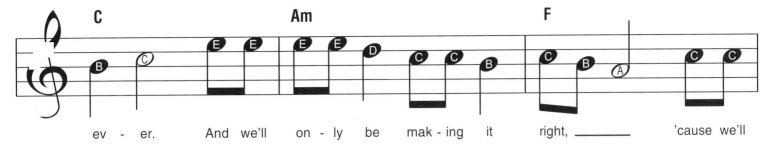

ev - er. And we'll on - ly be mak - ing it right, _____ 'cause we'll

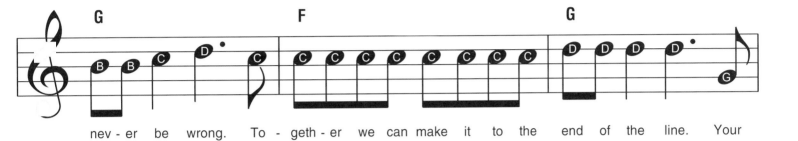

nev - er be wrong. To - geth - er we can make it to the end of the line. Your

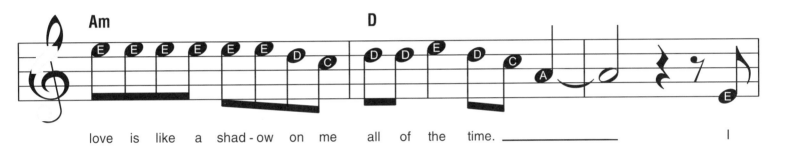

love is like a shad - ow on me all of the time. _____ I

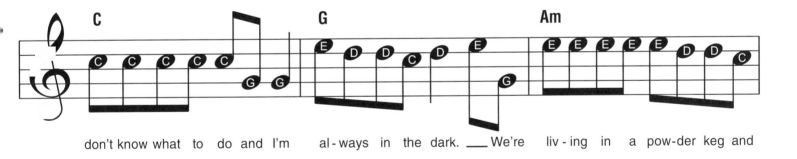

don't know what to do and I'm al - ways in the dark. ___ We're liv - ing in a pow - der keg and

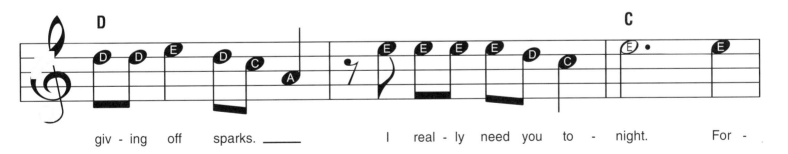

giv - ing off sparks. _____ I real - ly need you to - night. For -

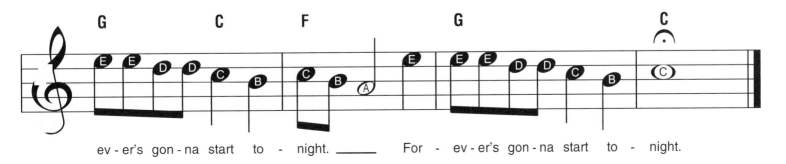

ev - er's gon - na start to - night. _____ For - ev - er's gon - na start to - night.

Unexpected Song
from SONG & DANCE

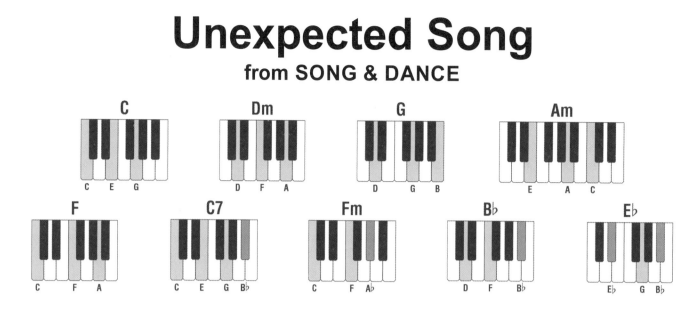

Music by Andrew Lloyd Webber
Lyrics by Don Black

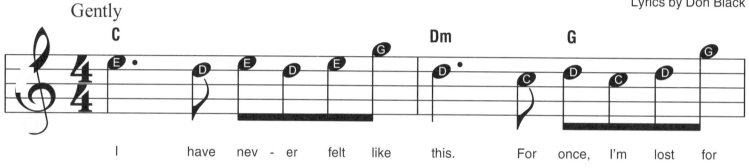

I have nev-er felt like this. For once, I'm lost for

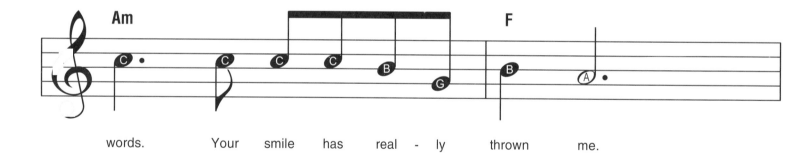

words. Your smile has real-ly thrown me.

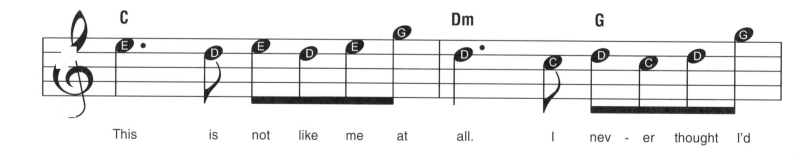

This is not like me at all. I nev-er thought I'd

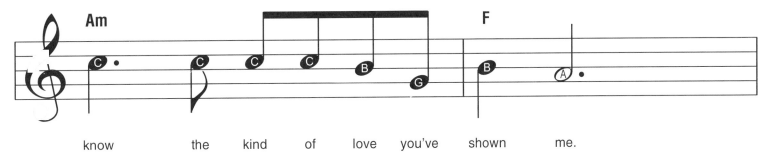

know   the   kind   of   love   you've shown   me.

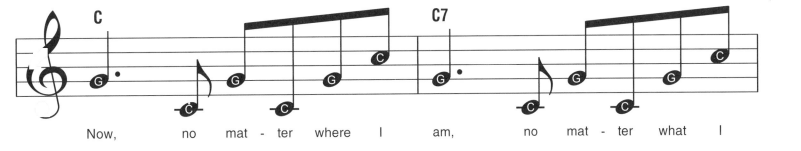

Now,   no   mat - ter   where   I   am,   no   mat - ter   what   I

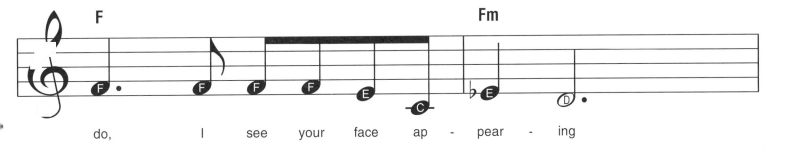

do,   I   see   your   face   ap -   pear - ing

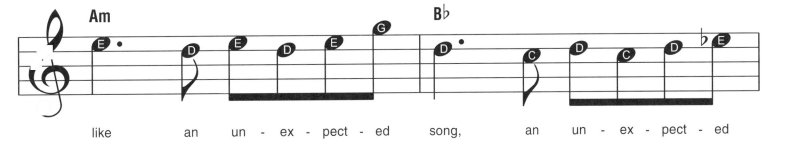

like   an   un -   ex -   pect - ed   song,   an   un -   ex -   pect - ed

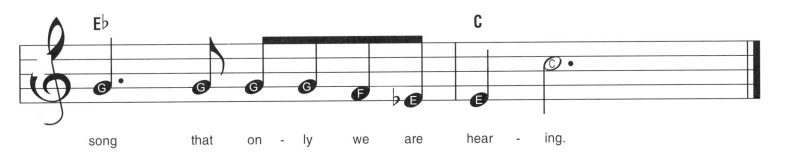

song   that   on -   ly   we   are   hear - ing.

When I Fall in Love
from ONE MINUTE TO ZERO

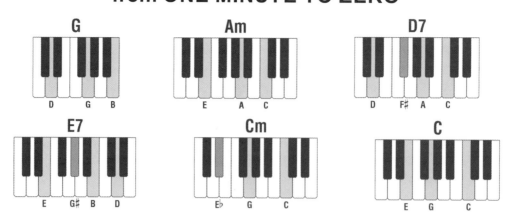

Words by Edward Heyman
Music by Victor Young

Moderately

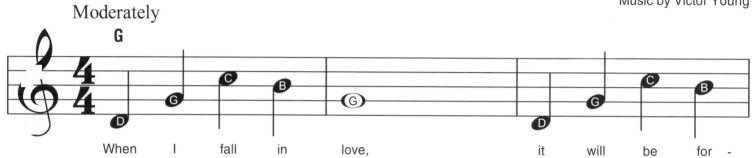

When I fall in love, it will be for -

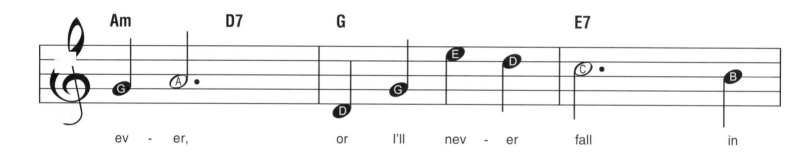

ev - er, or I'll nev - er fall in

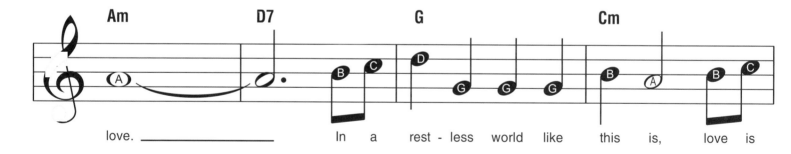

love. In a rest - less world like this is, love is

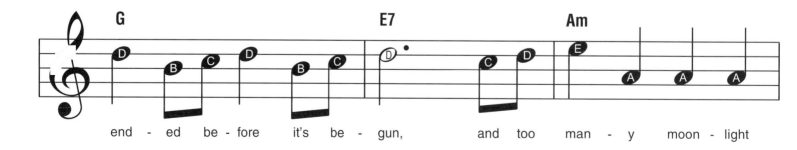

end - ed be - fore it's be - gun, and too man - y moon - light

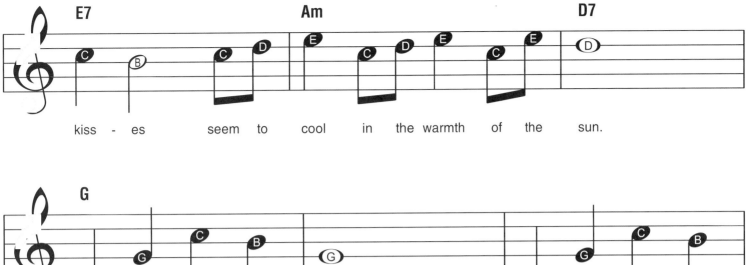

kiss - es   seem to   cool   in the warmth of the sun.

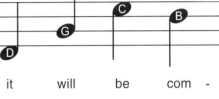

When I give my heart,   it will be com -

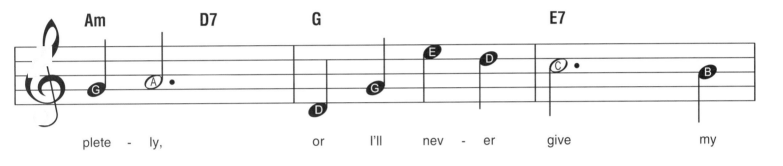

plete - ly,   or I'll nev - er give   my

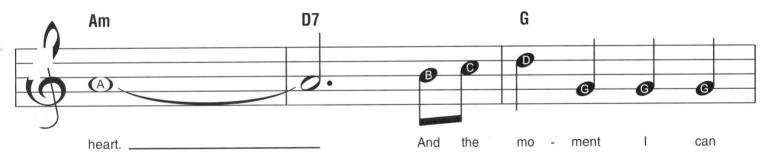

heart. _____   And the mo - ment I can

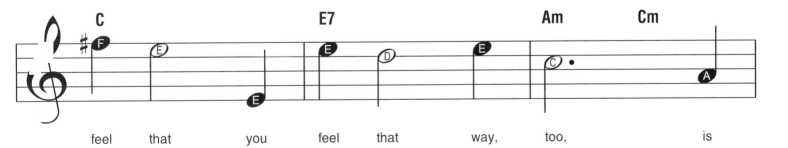

feel that   you   feel   that   way, too,   is

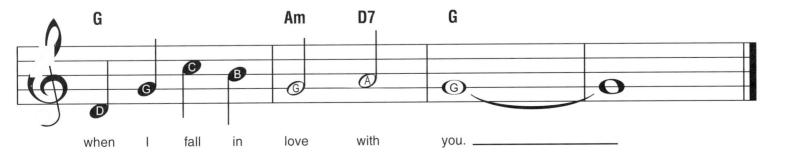

when I fall in love with   you. _____

When I Was Your Man

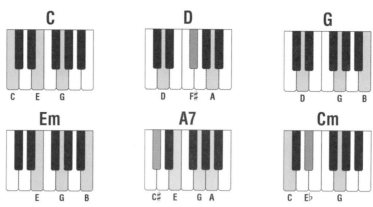

Words and Music by Bruno Mars,
Ari Levine, Philip Lawrence
and Andrew Wyatt

Moderately
(no chord)

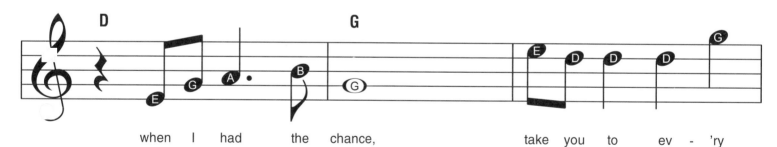

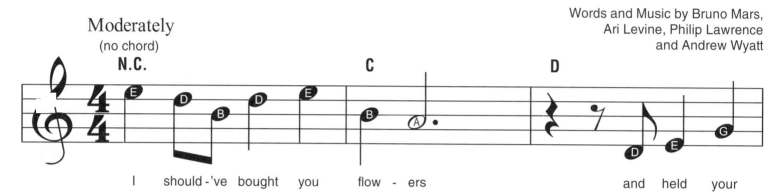

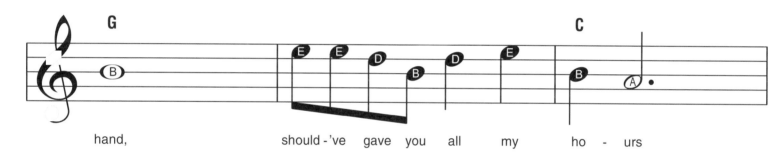

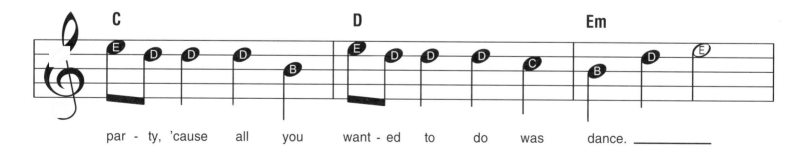

I should-'ve bought you flow-ers and held your hand, should-'ve gave you all my ho-urs when I had the chance, take you to ev-'ry par-ty, 'cause all you want-ed to do was dance. _____

A Whole New World

from ALADDIN

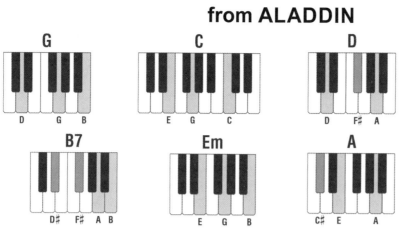
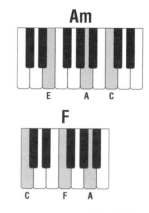

Music by Alan Menken
Lyrics by Tim Rice

Moderately

I can show you the world, shin - ing, shim - mer - ing,
I can o - pen your eyes, take you won - der by

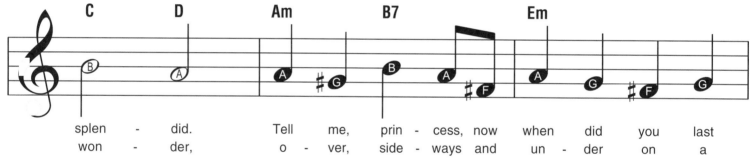

splen - did. Tell me, prin - cess, now when did you last
won - der, o - ver, side - ways and un - der on a

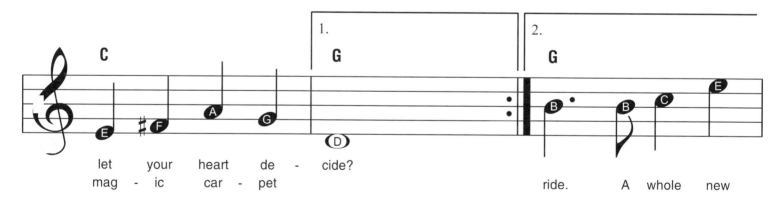

let your heart de - cide?
mag - ic car - pet ride. A whole new

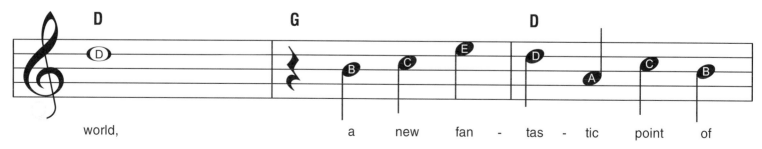

world, a new fan - tas - tic point of

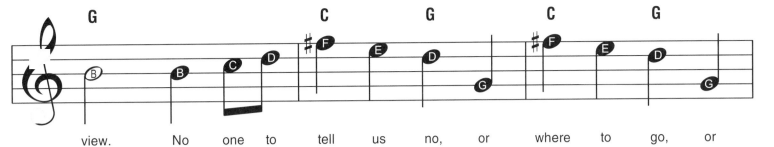

view. No one to tell us no, or where to go, or

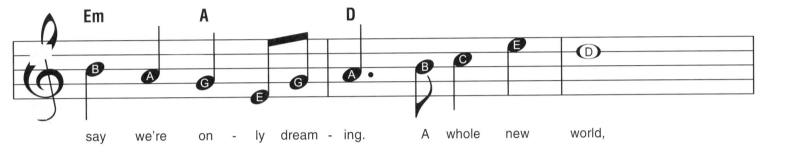

say we're on - ly dream - ing. A whole new world,

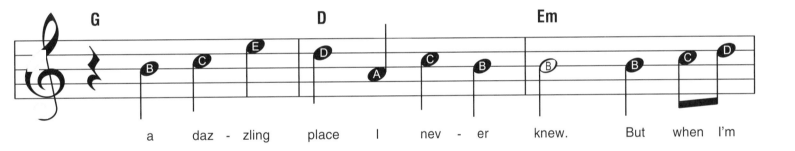

a daz - zling place I nev - er knew. But when I'm

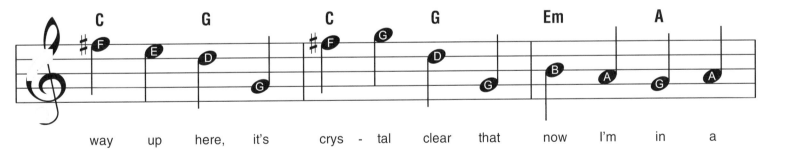

way up here, it's crys - tal clear that now I'm in a

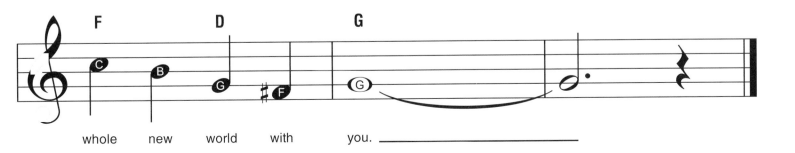

whole new world with you. _____

You Light Up My Life

from YOU LIGHT UP MY LIFE

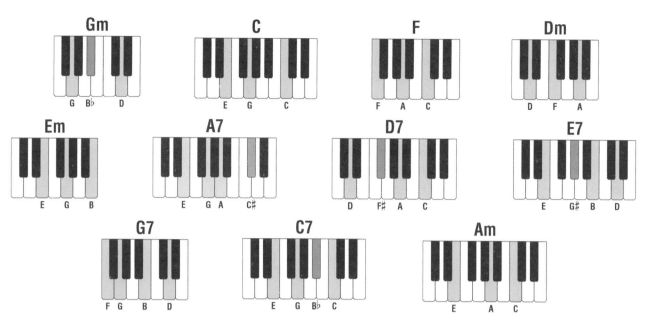

Words and Music by
Joseph Brooks

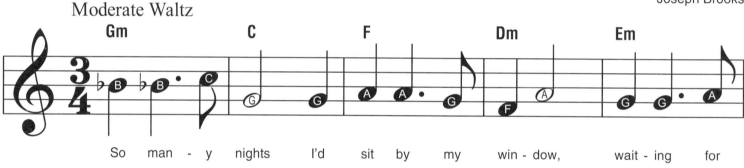

So man - y nights I'd sit by my win - dow, wait - ing for

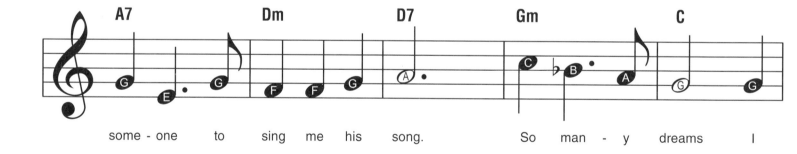

some - one to sing me his song. So man - y dreams I

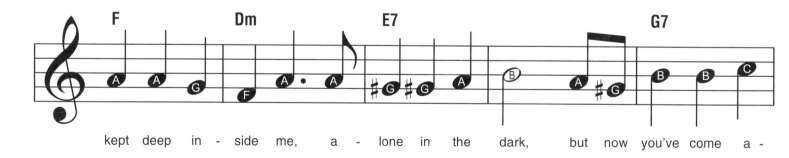

kept deep in - side me, a - lone in the dark, but now you've come a -

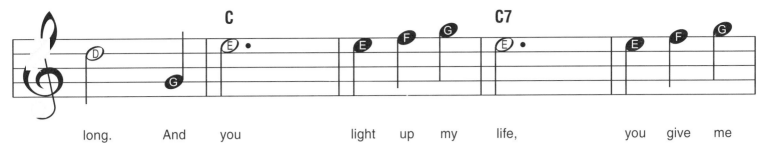

long. And you light up my life, you give me

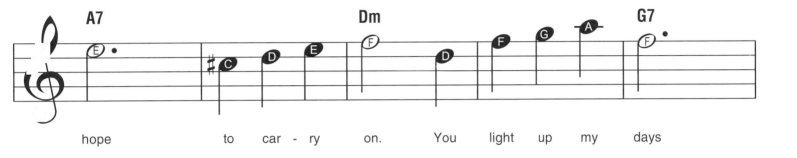

hope to car - ry on. You light up my days

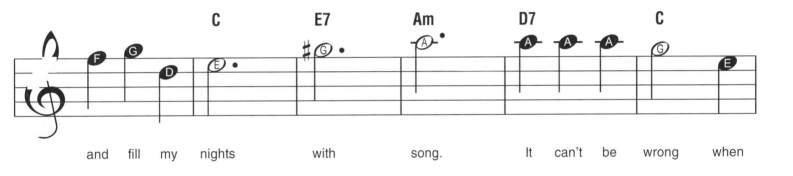

and fill my nights with song. It can't be wrong when

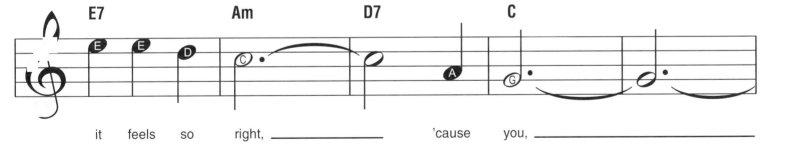

it feels so right, _____ 'cause you, _____

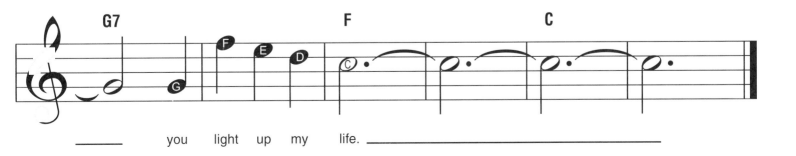

_____ you light up my life. _____